CREATIVE
FREEDOM

CREATIVE FREEDOM

Vocation of Liberal Religion

HENRY NELSON WIEMAN

CREIGHTON PEDEN
and LARRY E. AXEL
Editors

The Pilgrim Press
New York

Library of Congress Cataloging in Publication Data
Wieman, Henry Nelson, 1884-
Creative freedom, vocation of liberal religion.
Originally published in serial form beginning 1981:
American journal of theology & philosophy, ISSN 0194-3448.
Includes bibliographical references.
1. Freedom (Theology) 2. Liberalism (Religion)—History of
doctrines—20th century. 3. Wieman, Henry Nelson, 1884-
I. Peden, Creighton, 1935-   . II. Axel, Larry E., 1946-
III. Title. BT810.2.W47   1982   233'.7   82-10182
ISBN 0-8298-0623-7 (pbk.)

The Pilgrim Press, 132 West 31 Street, New York, New York 10001

CONTENTS

PREFACE

In writing *Creative Freedom: Vocation of Liberal Religion* Henry Nelson Wieman was at work in the 1950s on issues that may be even more relevant and urgent today, when authoritarian and parochial forms of religion are on the rise. Wieman argues that mature religion must assist people to realize the constructive possibilities of creativity and of their own uniqueness. Such a religion offers a renewed vision of the life of freedom--not only "freedom from," but also "freedom to"--and a more fulfilling life of creative transformation.

In this book Wieman seeks answers to the following significant questions: What kind of freedom ought religion attempt to nourish? When is freedom a mistaken goal? In contrast to popular misconceptions, what truly makes a religion "liberal"? When is religious tolerance not a proper stance? He examines the kinds of interchange that are often exploited in modern society, including manipulative, reiterative, and adaptive interchange, and he shows why these styles obstruct creativity. Wieman offers guidelines for achieving creative interchange, through realizing a new kind of human community and through a more mature awareness of "spiritual resources." One of the vocations of liberal religion is to utilize spiritual resources, that is, the meaning attached to symbols which can increase the dimension of creative interchange in people's lives.

Wieman notes, of course, that this enterprise is not merely a "spiritual" one; it is engaged fully in the everyday life of institutions and actions. If mature religion is to flourish in these times, it is essential that religious people understand the question of power in modern society and that the current alienation between education and religion be overcome. He examines these questions in detail and offers hope for developing a faith that will make religion a helpful and relevant force for contemporary humanity.

The original manuscript for *Creative Freedom* is part of the Henry Nelson Wieman Papers held in the Special Collections, Southern Illinois University. It was available only to researchers until 1981, when the *American Journal of Theology & Philosophy* began to publish it in serial form. Now, with the cooperation of The Pilgrim Press, we are pleased to make this work available to a wider audience.

We have edited the original manuscript in some places to avoid sexist terminology and awkward phraseology. We are confident this would have been Wieman's style had he lived long enough to have been made conscious of these more inclusive and sensitive forms of usage. In all cases we have sought to adhere rigidly to Wieman's essential meaning and have preserved the manuscript in literal form wherever this goal has been in any doubt.

We are grateful to many people for their help in bringing this book to fruition. Laura Wieman kindly granted publication permission and encouragement to the project. Carolyn Vickers and Tracy Reifel offered valuable secretarial assistance. Andy Hughes, David Mount, Scott Stevens, and Roy Evritt provided the technical skills necessary to transform the material into print. At various stages Kathy Coder and Keith Mohler volunteered typing and proofreading service. Finally, we are indebted to The Pilgrim Press for its support of this project and to the members of its staff, Marion M. Meyer and Arthur Hamparian, who guided *Creative Freedom* to publication.

Creighton Peden
Larry E. Axel

CREATIVE
FREEDOM

CHAPTER 1
Defending Freedom

Freedom and democracy are in decline. They can be revived and empowered but not if we shut our eyes to the danger and the problem. According to Walter Lippmann the loss of prestige, power, leadership and confidence once possessed by the democracies has been catastrophic, continuing for half a century.* Lands proclaiming freedom as their prized possession still have wealth, technology and private initiative beyond other people. But their domain is shrinking. The unquestioned world-leadership which they had in 1900 is slipping from them. Since the First World War millions have repudiated the ways of freedom. Today the people of the United States are afraid of traitors and enemies of freedom in their own homeland. They fear that democracy may be betrayed by fellow Americans as well as by enemies in other lands. One country after another has abandoned democracy in the sense in which the Western world understands democracy. Freedom has been retreating before the advance of the totalitarian powers.

All this is a complete reversal of the state of affairs in 1900. Beginning with the French and American revolutions at the turn of the nineteenth century democracy advanced in triumph for a hundred years. One country after another

* Walter Lippmann, *The Public Philosophy* (Boston: Little, Brown and Company, 1955).

adopted the slogans of freedom and the forms of democratic control. At the beginning of the twentieth century all the world looked to the democratic powers for leadership and for instruction in the ways of confidence, power, private initiative and respect for the individual. Never was democracy so highly honored and its power throughout the world so great. Almost everyone seemed to feel that the world would adopt the economy, the political forms and the aims of education developed in the West. It was generally believed that humanity at last had found the way of life to follow toward its highest attainment.

The contrast between 1905 and the present is almost unbelievable. The triumphant march and the confident outlook have been reversed. Weakness and decay have set in. Fear and uncertainty about the security of democracy even in its own homeland are eating into the minds of the devotees of freedom. The material resources and all the instruments and skills of mastery are with us still. No other culture and no other people can compare with the West in this respect. We have the tools for the exercise of supreme power. Indeed, we have never before had, and no other people ever has had, such resources in trained minds and material goods. But we seem unable to use them effectively against opposing powers. The hand has lost its cunning and the mind to direct the hand no longer has the vision and the insight.

Cause of the Decline of Freedom

What is the cause of this decline? Following in the tradition of many who have been observing and analyzing this development for over half a century, the cause can be summarized very briefly although full understanding leads into great complexities.

Put into most abbreviated form the cause of this decline

might be stated thus: The democratic peoples have come to interpret freedom in terms of private, local, competing and transitory interests. They view democracy as a utility to serve these interests and to raise the standard of living. They do not recognize as commanding their ultimate allegiance a common good underlying these private interests and sustaining them. They do not recognize the prior claim upon their devotion of that development continuous through history which creates freedom in social relations and in the mind of humanity. Having no such ultimate commitment the democratic peoples identify freedom with social control exercised by changing desires, hates and fears which happen at any time to possess the minds of individuals and the voting majority. Under such conditions the leaders of democratic society cannot command great sacrifice for what preserves freedom when its demands run counter to private interests and popular slogans. This results in a disastrous weakening of the power for concerted action in the struggle for dominance between freedom and tyranny.

This prevailing state of mind makes it impossible for those in positions of supreme command in the democratic societies to control the resources of the people according to knowledge, insight and counsel available to them. They must deal with problems subtle, complex and extending through long periods of history. But they must shape their policies and interpret their actions to conform to the demands of special interests, organized groups and transitory passions. Minds obsessed with these interests and passions are in no position to understand what needs to be done to protect the historic continuity of what underlies and sustains their private interests. However, those in positions of responsibility with access to information and counsel which enable them to understand better what needs to be done, cannot govern in a way to protect and promote what creates and sustains the free society. They cannot because they must shape their course of action to conform to the demands of minds which have neither understanding of, nor compelling allegiance to, the underlying and vital needs of freedom.

This is the predicament of the democracies. This is the cause of their weakness and decay according to many analysts. For this reason the democracies are in retreat before the totalitarian powers and cannot act with the decision, skill and wisdom to hold their own against the rising tide of tyranny. There is something going on in human life, continuous throughout history, which creates the free society and the free individual when allegiance is given to it and when those in positions of authority can command the resources of the people to serve, protect and promote it. Social policy might be shaped in its service; concerted action and great sacrifice might be commanded for its defense and for meeting its demands. But until this basic, sustaining and creative good is recognized and given the place of priority the free society cannot defend its freedom when sacrifices of private interests must be made. In such times of peril those in positions of highest responsibility have not the authority to command when private interests determine what shall be commanded.

This popular blindness to the common good and public interest is increased in our time by the interpretation given to the conflict with communism and the totalitarian powers. Our enemies glorify a common good which submerges the needs and interests of the individual. Therefore, so it is said, we must magnify the unique and diverse demands of individuals, the competing and transitory goals of endeavor which happen to be most popular, the local and private interests of individuals and organized groups. But this is a false alternative. There is a common good which underlies the aggregate of private interests and sustains the free society. This is what the government should serve and protect above all else and not the aggregate of private interests.

Certainly this good which is common to all is not the state nor the economic determinism of history nor anything which submerges the individual. On the contrary it liberates the individual and magnifies his or her importance and power. But it does this for everyone and therefore is a common good. Consequently it is prior in importance to the changing desires of the conscious minds of those not concerned about it. Its imperative demands remain no matter how they are misinterpreted or ignored. Therefore to interpret the needs of the social system of freedom in terms of the prevailing concerns of conscious minds which ignore these needs is to betray the social system. This is the weakness of the democracies. It has caused them to fall disastrously in fifty years from their place of leadership in world affairs.

The Source of Freedom

If there is any truth in this analysis and interpretation of our predicament it calls for a deeper search into the nature and source of freedom. In proceeding to do this we leave Lippmann because we do not think that his constructive suggestions are as profound or as true as his diagnosis of the problem to be solved. The problem is to find what calls for the ultimate allegiance of those who fight for freedom; what calls for the sacrifice of private interests in service of the common good and public interest; what the government should protect and promote, not by obeying groups within the body politic, but by commanding these all in concerted action to serve what is deeper and greater and more precious than their demands.

Local groups and private interests must be represented in

the government; they must be considered and served. But to serve these private interests and follow the guidance of the uninformed man or woman on the street in a way to destroy the sources of freedom is to serve the people treacherously even when the treachery is unintended.

Perhaps the source and nature of freedom will emerge most clearly into view if we examine a very simple case. Consider a man giving his money at the point of a gun. The robber says, Give me your money or your life. I quickly hand my money over. I do this voluntarily. I choose to give my money; my own will so decides. But this is not freedom. It is not because a part of myself resists and rebels against what another part of myself actually does. In some cases my entire conscious mind can act willingly and yet the deep unconscious levels of the mind resist bitterly what the conscious level is doing.

What, then, is freedom? It is the whole self in action. It is any decision or any action which satisfies the whole self and not merely one part or level of the mind. In that sense, perhaps, no human being is ever completely free but we can all have degrees of freedom. Freedom can be increased indefinitely. We never have complete and perfect freedom because the demands of the total self are greater than any action can satisfy. In a sense it is humankind's glory that its potentialities exceed the capacities of the world to satisfy them at any time. On that account we are the transformers of the world toward greater good when we seek and act with understanding of what the greater good truly is. But we must understand what truly satisfies our nature in its wholeness and not merely some transitory interest which happens to possess the conscious mind at a given time. Perhaps the most difficult and ultimate wisdom is to understand what would satisfy the undivided self in its wholeness.

Freedom and Coercion

Freedom is not the absence of coercion. Let us turn again to the man at the point of the gun to see how coercion can be absorbed in such a way as to issue in freedom. Suppose that I give my money to the robber without any inner resistance of any kind. Suppose that I deliver the money with my whole self in action, with every level of the mind supporting the act. Suppose I understand and accept all the consequences of this action willingly without suppression or inhibition. That would be freedom. Such action may seem fantastic at the point of a gun, but Socrates died with that kind of freedom under the coercions of the Athenian republic. So have others met coercion with freedom in this way.

To some degree we all act freely under coercion at times. I obey the traffic rules at the point of a gun, so to speak, since the police officers are ready to arrest me if I do not. Nevertheless in most cases I obey freely. We often obey the rules of courtesy without inner resistance and with the whole self in the act so far as that is humanly possible although, if we think about it, we know that society would cast us out if we did not observe the rules of decency. In that sense a person acts at the point of a gun although freely. Parents often sacrifice for their children with the whole self in the act although they know that if they did not, society would severely condemn them in some cases.

The point of these illustrations is to show that every human being from infancy absorbs innumerable coercions into his or her own individuality so that they become habits and impulses and are enacted without inner resistance, always remembering the reservations that this is never done completely and perfectly. Freedom at the human level is impossible without absorbing many coercions in this way. One must learn to talk correctly, to read and write. In early childhood one must undergo toilet training and acquire under more or less coercion all the other rules of behavior without which one cannot be accepted into society. These coercions continue more or less throughout the entire life of every individual because without them the human mind, with its understanding and use of the language and other symbols and with logical forms of thinking would not come into existence or operate. Without these coercions organized society would be impossible and no culture could be accumulated and conserved.

Freedom, then, is not the absence of coercions but it is the way we deal with coercions. There are two ways of dealing with coercions in freedom. One is to absorb them into the organization of the personality after the manner mentioned so that they become assets and endowments, expanding the range of what one can know, feel and control; developing the powers of insight and understanding of other minds; increasing the capacity for mutual control between equals and reducing the need for authoritarian control exercised by superiors over inferiors.

The second way of dealing with coercion is to resist it to the point of defeat with full knowledge of the consequences and with full acceptance of them. To resist coercion with the whole undivided self in action to the point of death and to do this without inner resistance to what the conscious mind does, is freedom in the face of overwhelming coercion. This is possible only if this something deeper satisfies the whole self even while one is succumbing to superior power.

We speak of freedom in defeat when fighting a coercion which cannot be conquered. It is truly defeat in the sense that the coercion prevails over resistance; but if triumph means to find the most profound satisfaction of the whole self by reason of devotion to what ultimately satisfies the nature of humankind, then in that sense it is not defeat but triumph. In any case it is freedom when freedom is understood to be the whole self in action.

Again a previous statement must be reiterated because it

plays a very important part in the further development of this understanding of freedom and yet may seem to be contradicted or obscured when we speak of instances in which freedom is attained. The human person in the wholeness of his or her being is never completely unified. The unified, harmonized self acting with all its resources free from inner restraint is a condition which may be more or less remotely approximated. To the degree that it is approached we have freedom. In this sense it is correct to speak of having attained freedom, meaning that degree of approximation to integrated wholeness of the self in action which is the maximum possible under the present conditions of human existence.

As Freud says, there is always a residual part of the self called the id, which is not transformed in a way to act with that part which is shaped and guided by language and the other signs and symbols of the culture. This is not altogether the fault of the evil id; and on this point Freud is disputed by many psychologists today. It is also the fault of the culture. The demands of the culture and of the organization of society can be improved in the sense that more of the individual's total capacity for response can be developed or harmonized with the level of conscious life and civilized existence. Perhaps no culture and no social order and no possible perfection in the rearing of children can ever develop the human person in such a way as to leave no residual unsocialized part. Always there is an id to resist the demands of the most inclusive purpose ever to be conceived by any human mind. But a culture and a social order might be developed in such a way that this uncivilized part of the self could be drawn into the culture more or less continuously to realize further potentialities of human life. In such case the id, instead of being shut out completely, could be a kind of reserve of undeveloped humanity, to be developed when social demands make it possible to realize these further potentialities of human existence.

Social Conditions and Creative Transformation

This interpretation of the problem of freedom reaches down into the depth of human nature and points up toward the supreme fulfillment of all the constructive potentialities of the individual person. Freedom is had to the degree that the individual person in the wholeness of her or his being is acting in such a way as to undergo this kind of creative transformation of the whole self--so far as wholeness can be achieved--in such a way as to increase the range of knowledge, power of control, aesthetic experience, appreciative understanding of other minds and capacity for mutual control as over against authoritarian control.

The creative transformation of the mind is the work of a creativity which feeds on the sort of interchange producing appreciative understanding of the unique individuality of each and consequent learning in depth from each other. Learning in depth means learning with the whole self so far as the self has attained wholeness. It also means learning from the whole self of the other so far as the other is able to express an undivided self. This kind of learning results in creative transformation of the whole mind and not merely a bit of added skill or information.

This, then, is the problem to solve when we undertake to guard and promote freedom. The problem is, on the one hand, to provide social conditions most favorable for the kind of interchange and creativity just mentioned. On the other hand, the problem is to have the kind of religious commitment which commands the ultimate allegiance of the whole self in the struggle to provide or develop these social conditions. The kind of religious commitment required to do this, I shall try to show, is a mature form of liberal religion. But just now let us look at the social conditions which are needed.

The simplified conditions of childhood enable us to see more clearly than in the complexities of later life the social relations in which freedom can grow. At this level, as at all other levels in the development of the individual, the social problem of freedom can be viewed as that of applying coercions in a way to increase rather than diminish freedom. Otherwise stated, it is the problem of applying coercions in a way to bring about creative transformation of the mind.

In the relation between parent and child this social problem of freedom is solved to the degree that the parents achieve appreciative understanding of the mind of the child and are thereby able to impose coercions in such a way that the child can absorb them into the organization of his or her own personality. When this is done the coercions are transformed into resources for living and enlarge the freedom of the individual. If this is not done, the coercions produce the inner conflict which limits freedom. This inner conflict limits capacity to appreciate and enjoy, to solve problems, to achieve insight into the minds of other people and understand them. It distorts perception, impairs rational coherence and blocks many an intuition which might otherwise show the way through difficulties. The free individual is one who has command of all the resources for human living. Inner conflict limits freedom because it limits this command of personal resources.

Not only in the relation between parent and child but in every interpersonal relation throughout society at all ages the one primary social condition of freedom is readiness to engage in the kind of interchange which produces appreciative understanding of the unique individuality of one another. This readiness and this capacity to attain appreciative understanding depends in turn upon all major institutions such as the family, the school, industry and business, government and the religion of the churches. If these are all so ordered and conducted as to provide conditions most favorable for the kind of interchange producing the understanding mentioned, there will be the highest degree of freedom.

This understanding of one another in depth occurs when the whole self responds with sensitivity and attentiveness to every expression of the other person. This will occur to the measure that people give their whole selves over to this kind of interchange, giving it priority over every other claim made upon them. People will be able and willing to do this to the measure that they have developed from infancy in a way to attain this wholeness of the self and this commitment of the self; and this in turn depends upon the major institutions. The major institutions will be shaped to this end if the people are most completely committed to the undertaking of constructing them in this way. Thus there is a circle in which personality, commitment and social institutions all depend on one another. But the creative center of this circle is a religion which leads people to give themselves most fully to the work of shaping the institutions and interacting with one another in the ways mentioned.

Religious Commitment and Self-giving

Religion is here defined as commitment to what one believes to be of such character and power that it will transform human beings as they cannot transform themselves to save them from the worst and lead them to the best when required conditions are present, chief of these conditions being the most complete self-giving to it. This self-giving is called faith or religious commitment. A religion is good or bad, wise or foolish, depending on what is believed to have the character and power to save and transform as mentioned. It is here contended that what has this character and power is the creativity which rears the human mind in infancy and creatively transforms the mind in a way to realize the constructive potentialities of each unique individual. It is the creativity which produces appreciative understanding of one another when one gives oneself most completely to the interchange as above described. It is the creativity which enables each to learn in depth from the other and to absorb coercions in a way to increase freedom. It is also the reality which satisfies the self in such wholeness and depth that when completely devoted to it one can go down in defeat as described above and still be free and triumphant.

This creativity is the common good which underlies, creates and sustains all private interests and calls for the ultimate allegiance of every person, claiming priority of devotion and sacrifice over every other interest. The free society gathers power to resist its enemies, convert its foes and solve its problems when all the resources of the people can be commanded to defend and build the conditions required for this creativity to dominate over counter processes. The free society loses its power, inwardly decays and is defeated in conflict with its foes, when concerted action and massive sacrifice can only be commanded by appeal to some aggregate of private interests.

Ultimate allegiance given to this creativity because of the demonstrable truth that it has prior claim on the devotion of every person is a form of mature liberal religion. Liberal religion is understood to be one which accepts as its guiding beliefs only those which can be supported by reason and in that sense are demonstrable. Such a religion and no other can save freedom in its time of peril. But for liberal religion to do this it must develop a maturity it does not now have. This maturity of liberal religion will be discussed in the following pages. In the meantime the development of a mature faith of this kind requires that we rid ourselves of mistaken ideas about freedom. So to a critical examination of these ideas we turn in the next chapter.

CHAPTER 2
Mistaken Ideas of Freedom

Religious freedom is not a special kind of freedom which can be separated from other freedoms. Free religion is nothing else than a religion which provides for the freedom of the individual in the wholeness of his or her being. So with any other kind of freedom which might be mentioned. These so-called kinds of freedom are mentioned in the plural not because there are in truth different kinds of freedom but because there are different conditions which must be present to enable individuals to have freedom. These various conditions are called freedoms by a kind of figure of speech which is very common in ordinary language.

Four ideas of freedom, considered mistaken in this discussion, will be examined.

Freedom to Do as You Like

(1) People sometimes speak of freedom as though it meant to do as you like. But people often like to escape from freedom. They like to be enslaved to opium or alcohol. They like to be relieved of the responsibility of making decisions by accepting the dictates of some authority. Therefore if you say that freedom means to do as you like, you are saying that freedom means to be not free in such cases. To identify freedom with non-freedom is to land in utter confusion; yet this confusion is not at all uncommon.

Psychology of personality is full of descriptions of people

who escape from freedom. One of the most highly esteemed of psychologists and sociologists, Erich Fromm, has written a book entitled *Escape from Freedom*. This and other studies show that millions of people seek the opposite of freedom. In fact we all do at times. Consequently freedom cannot be identified with doing as you like. There is a kind of liking which leads to freedom; but since many likings lead to the opposite of freedom, any statement about freedom which obscures the distinction between the two is confusing.

Seeking the Truth

(2) There is another mistaken idea of freedom. It has to do with "seeking the truth." People sometimes speak as though they had freedom to seek the truth when they construct moral and religious beliefs to suit themselves. But constructing moral and religious beliefs to suit oneself is a way of seeking illusion and not truth. Truth, or, more accurately stated, knowledge which may approximate the truth, can be achieved only by the rigor and discipline of a method which detects the errors you cherish and compels you to accept statements supported by evidence whether they suit you or not. Nowhere is disciplined inquiry more difficult than in morals and religion. Nowhere is human desire and self-esteem and social bias more treacherous. The claim that each person can find the truth for himself or herself in this area but cannot find it in the exact sciences, simply is not true.

In seeking true statements to solve problems in science or morals or religion the right method must be used for distinguishing what is true from what is false. But something else is also needed which is even more difficult to achieve. It is getting the insight, hunch, clue or theory capable of being tested and developed into knowledge. Both of these two, the insight and the method, are necessary. Either one without the other is futile. The method is needed to test the insight, correct it and develop it to the point where it can be accepted as true and adequate to solve the problem. The insight is needed because without it you have nothing to test and develop into knowledge.

The method can simply be described thus: (1) Develop the implications of the insight to the point where you can know what must happen under given conditions if the insight is true; also what must happen under given conditions if it is false. (2) Seek out or set up these conditions and make your observations. For example, I have the hunch which might be called an insight, that the white stuff in the cup is salt. If it is, then under given conditions I will observe a certain distinctive taste. I set up the required conditions by touching my tongue to the salt. If further testing is required I subject the white stuff to chemical analysis. This is a more elaborate way of doing the same thing, although measured units rather than sense qualities are used in the exact sciences to test any theory.

With this understanding it is plain that when liberals construct their own religious beliefs without the needed insight and without competent application of the method and without the labor and discipline required to achieve such competence, these liberals are no more free than traditionalists. They have simply shifted from bondage to illusions sustained by a tradition to bondage to illusions constructed by themselves. Such illusions may be worse than those of a great tradition. Perhaps the greatest danger to freedom is the siren song of cherished beliefs which we want more than we want the austere truth. Casting off the authority of tradition in order to believe as you like is not the road to freedom.

Two kinds of authority should be distinguished. One is dogmatic. The other is the authority of a reliable method for detecting error and gathering evidence and the authority of those who use this method with competence after long and rigorous training. Authority of the first kind is the foe of freedom but the second is one necessary condition of freedom.

Uncaused Choice

(3) Freedom is not uncaused choice and uncaused action. The only kind of action anybody ever wants is action caused and guided by knowledge of conditions leading to anticipated consequences.

If action is not caused by knowledge of conditions and anticipated consequences, one is just as likely to jump off a high cliff as to jump off a six-inch platform. Choice and action which are free must be subject to causation if freedom is a great good to seek and cherish. The form of causation which appears in free choice and free action is different from other forms of causation. But to represent freedom as opposed to causation is to give the name of freedom to something which would swiftly bring all human life to an end. The causation which operates in freedom is the causation of action by knowledge of conditions and anticipated consequences plus the causation exercised by the organization of the total self so far as it is unified.

Tolerance Without Commitment

(4) Still another mistaken idea about freedom calls for examination. It is the error of thinking that freedom requires tolerance without a clearly defined limit of tolerance.

No people can be free and tolerate enslavement. Neither can they keep their freedom if they tolerate what will lead to tyranny. Tyranny can tolerate everything except freedom. Tyranny can be as tolerant as freedom, but with the

opposite principle defining the limits of tolerance. To asso-
ciate freedom and tolerance without stating the principle
distinguishing what can be tolerated from what cannot be,
is to render freedom defenseless against tyranny. Tyranny
can tolerate a great variety of persons and practices in the
sense of a great diversity of deceptions, frauds and tricks by
which a society is enslaved, and a great diversity of subtle
methods by which a people is kept in bondage, a great
diversity of disguises by which external forms of freedom
are used to conceal the actual presence of tyranny. A
tyranny which is intelligent, resourceful and potent must be
widely tolerant. A free society which is intelligent,
resourceful and potent must be widely tolerant. But no
society, whether enslaved or free, can be intelligent,
resourceful and potent if it is not very clear concerning the
principle distinguishing what can be tolerated and what
cannot be.

The principle determining the limits of tolerance with
freedom as here interpreted can be briefly stated. Everything should be tolerated which does not seriously obstruct
the interchange creative of mutual understanding between
individuals and peoples across the barrier of diverse views
and interests. Nothing should be tolerated which seriously
hinders such interchange unless suppressing it would hinder
this interchange even more than allowing the obstruction to
continue. The action of intolerance when such action is
required is not vicious attack. It is first of all doing everything possible to penetrate or overcome the barrier to
appreciative understanding which has been set up by those
who resist friendly relations. The most difficult but at
same time most imperative part of this undertaking is to
examine oneself and one's own society to see and correct
the barriers in ourselves. If the barriers cannot be overcome and if behind these barriers practices continue which
increasingly   tear   down   the   conditions   required   for

understanding one another, violence may be necessary. For example we use violence to confine criminals and the insane because such action will not diminish mutual trust and appreciative interchange among people so much as would be the case if such persons were allowed to continue at large. When and where and how violence should be used must be determined by the consequences issuing from it. If the consequences of violence should impair the conditions needed for creative interchange more seriously than leaving matters stand, then violence should not be used. Obviously the complexities of life will often make it very difficult to decide when to use violence and when not; but the principle is clear however obscure may be the demands of the concrete situation. Guiding principles we must have no matter how difficult their application to concrete situations. Without such guiding principles the cause of freedom, or any other cause for that matter, is hopelessly lost.

Creative interchange as guiding principle does not mean that every individual can practice it with every other person in society. Obviously that is impossible. It does mean, however, that every individual shall be in readiness to practice it whenever contact, problem or difficulty require it. This is another way of saying that ultimate commitment to creative interchange must be the prevailing religion if freedom is to be saved and is to grow amid social conditions now developing.

Tolerance without this commitment creates a form of deception in the relations between people. The relation is deceptive because those who claim to tolerate others without understanding their true individuality and without any opportunity or effort to understand are not tolerating true individuals at all but only dummies. Those who tolerate in this way are deceiving both themselves and the other persons.

Tolerance without this commitment is dangerous because

the persons tolerated may be driven by malicious and destructive impulses. Malice and destructiveness can be tolerated within limits when we have understanding of them because we can then be on our guard or exercise needed control. But without this understanding the society cannot protect itself nor can any individual associated with such a person or practice.

Tolerance without this commitment is impoverishing to all concerned. Most of the enrichment of human life comes from apprehending what others appreciate beyond my own vision and learning to appreciate what the mind of the other opens to me. Even the most evil of persons as well as the righteous can open up depths and fullness of experience, as all great works of fiction indicate. But this can happen only if there is understanding of such a person. Tolerance without this is impoverishing and reduces human association to a kind of sterile knocking about like so many billiard balls.

Tolerance without prevailing commitment of this kind is always on the verge of envy, jealousy, malice, hate and fear because it is almost impossible for human beings in association to remain indifferent to one another. This is the danger hanging over the world at the present time when all the races, cultures and peoples must live together in close association. Either they must accept a religion of commitment to creative interchange producing appreciative understanding of one another or else envy, jealousy, hate and fear will mount to the point of destructive conflict and devastation.

The psychological study of human personality has shown that when people are intensely aware of being not understood and appreciated by associates and do not themselves understand others, they resort to various practices. One is aggression and destructive violence. Another is suppression of their own individuality to the point where they become automatic mechanisms conforming to the dictates of superficial social convention where everyone parrots the same thoughts and feelings. Still other devices are practiced which have been elaborately described by the psychologists. The point concerning them all is to show that tolerance without commitment to creativity reduces freedom to the minimum, when freedom is understood to be the total unified self in action in such a way as to realize progressively the constructive potentialities of each human being. Therefore we cannot be free if we tolerate conditions, practices and attitudes which seriously hinder the appreciative understanding of one another.

An Ultimate Commitment

So far the mistaken ideas about freedom which we have considered have been errors of omission. The next to be examined is one of insufficiency.

If freedom is to survive and grow under social conditions now developing, the commitment to creative interchange must be ultimate in the sense that nothing else can take priority over it. This ultimacy of the commitment is required for many reasons but one only will here be mentioned.

The commitment must be ultimate to keep anxiety under control. As has already been said and will be developed more fully in following pages, anxiety increases as society becomes more complex, social change accelerates and associates become more diversified and transitory. Anxiety in this context does not mean fear of some definable object. It is the distress arising from the feeling that one may lose the respect of associates as well as self-respect. That is the way one psychologist describes it. Others describe it as arising from the recognition that the depth of subjectivity in oneself is unknown, ignored, unsustained by one's associates.

Or again it can be called the feeling that this total self which I am with all its hidden memories, aspirations, joys and sorrows, has no meaning or purpose or value because it cannot be expressed or made to serve any form of action nor win recognition from any one. This anxiety is complex and is variously interpreted by different psychologists and philosophers and theologians. Also to some degree it is kept out of consciousness even when unconsciously operative to disrupt social relations and derange the organization of personality. The intensity and danger of this anxiety seem to grow with increasing diversity and rapid changes of social contacts unless brought under control by the right kind of religious commitment.

The danger is that this depth and wholeness of the self beyond the reach of social recognition and appreciation will seem to be worthless, a bit of waste accidentally thrown off by the waves of change which have brought human beings into existence. This inability to value what is distinctively human in oneself will make it impossible to value the depth of subjectivity in others. This generates the anxiety mentioned. To keep the torment of this anxiety out of mind people do monstrous things; they become demonic as recent history demonstrates. This state of mind increases and becomes more dangerous when self-consciousness increases if corrective commitment is not practiced. Self-consciousness increases when the contrast between oneself and others is magnified. This contrast makes one more aware of the peculiar being which is oneself, so uniquely different from every other. This contrast is continuously magnified as increasing social complexity and change bring the individual into contact with more different kinds of people. Also a mechanized form of social organization seems to cast off as worthless ever more of the unique subjective depth of the individual--hence the rising danger in a society becoming more complex, more diversified and rapidly changing.

Keeping this anxiety under control means to keep it from developing self-destructive and socially destructive propensities which always arise when it is not properly treated. This anxiety is properly treated when social interchange gives to the individual a sense of the supreme preciousness of the total hidden subjectivity which is her or his own true self and the true self of every other human being. This can be done by nothing less than an ultimate commitment to what does in truth reveal the precious value of the total hidden self. This revelation occurs when one gives herself or himself most completely to the kind of interchange which produces appreciative understanding of one another to whatever maximum degree is possible.

Such commitment reveals the precious value of the total self first of all because it brings more of the subjectivity to the level where others can recognize it. This results when one devotes all one's resources to sustaining and improving the conditions for mutual appreciation. In the second place commitment to creativity reveals the precious value of the total self because it brings more of the subjectivity into action and self-expression and thus gives to this subjectivity the value of such action. In the third place commitment to the creative transformation of humanity reveals the precious value of the total self because it is precisely the depth of subjectivity not yet brought into action and recognition which makes it possible for human life to undergo improvement beyond any known limit. This is so because improvement means development of language and art, of personal relations and institutions, of nervous energy and health, of devotion and purity of heart, such that more of the hidden potentialities of the self can come to recognition and constructive action. The presence of these potentialities in the hidden and unused depths of subjectivity is what makes possible the fuller realization of human good.

Thus the hidden, socially unrecognized and unexpressed depth of the total self ceases to be waste and loss takes on transcendent value because it is the promise of all creative transformation which can ever occur. This promise gives maximum preciousness to the hidden and unused and unexpressed depth of my own subjective self and likewise for every other individual. Each individual takes on a preciousness far beyond anything this person says or does. Also if one gives oneself completely to this creativity, rare moments will occur when the total self seems to reach the level of constructive action, full expression and unrestrained appreciation. In such moments this may shine forth in others and rise to ecstasy in oneself.

For all these reasons commitment to creativity can bring under control the anxiety which threatens self-destruction and social disaster when not thus controlled. But nothing short of religious commitment can do this. Any lesser degree of self-giving will allow other passions to take command. Every human drive other than this commitment and uncontrolled by it, leaves the subjectivity at the deeper levels of the total mind unused, unvalued and unsustained. This brings on the feeling that human existence has no meaning sufficiently important to make life worth living. The consequent despair and intensified anxiety get out of control leading to self-destructive and socially destructive action. This produces conditions which augment the despair and anxiety. Thus the destructive dialectic gets under way and the vicious circle rolls toward the abyss.

We have looked at five different ideas about freedom which we believe are misleading. The first four are: "freedom" to do as you like, "freedom" to believe as you like, "freedom" to choose outside the chain of cause and effect, and "freedom" which tolerates without defined limits of tolerance. Finally we have tried to show that any attempt to guard and promote freedom under conditions now developing will end in failure and disaster if it is not based upon a religion of ultimate commitment to creativity. This creativity demands the freest and fullest interchange between persons and peoples, thus expanding and deepening appreciative understanding by each of the other. Also it deepens appreciation of the transcendent value resident in the depth of subjectivity which is one's total self and the total self of others.

CHAPTER 3
Freedom and Individualism

One kind of individualism is described by David Riesman in his book *The Lonely Crowd*. The person who exemplifies it is called the "inner-directed person," by Riesman. "Inner-directed" may be an unfortunate term, but Riesman gives it a special meaning of his own. Therefore, those who have used "inner-directed" exclusively as a laudatory term should not object to the special meaning given it by Riesman so long as he makes plain that his usage is not laudatory but purely descriptive.

The inner-directed person is one who acquires an ideal in childhood or youth from family members and other intimate associates and holds it throughout life. Such a person not only holds it; his or her developing personality is shaped by it. This ideal may be to achieve success in the form of great wealth; or an ideal of success may be performance of the perfect crime. Again it may be to become a great poet or preacher or political leader or whatever. The point is that the inner-directed person subordinates everything to the achievement of a personal ideal.

In our American tradition it is common to think of life conducted in this way as the noblest. It is thought to be a most admirable kind of moral idealism if the chosen ideal is one generally approved in our society. But here important distinctions must be made which are often overlooked, and Riesman's penetrating analysis exposes them.

No abstract ideal can comprehend the richness and

fullness of appreciations, habits, impulses and interchanges which must enter into any way of life capable of developing the constructive potentialities of a human being. All the loves, loyalties, affections and vast wealth of spontaneous impulse enriching life at the human level far exceed the bounds of any intellectually formulated system of possibilities held up as an ideal. No construction of human thought can comprehend the richness and fullness of true individuality because all the constructions of the conscious intellect are only a small part of all which enters into the total human being. The scope and diversity of a fully developed life cannot be reduced · to the abstractions of human thought any more than all the vital processes of the biological organism can be reduced to the single function of the seeing eye.

The unfitness of every ideal to comprehend the fullness of life reveals the evil of striving to cramp and confine the total development of the individual into the limits of an ideal constructed by the mind in the immature days of youth. This is not the kind of individualism which makes for freedom because it prevents the whole self from acting and from undergoing that creative transformation which lifts life from infancy to the level of fully developed humanity. With this kind of individualism the preacher, the lawyer, the doctor, the person of research, the teacher and everyone else becomes a professional stereotype. One becomes a mechanism for embodying an ideal instead of a true person with all the endowments of human living.

No matter how noble the ideal and no matter how faithfully devoted to it one may be, the inner-directed person lacks integrity because no ideal can contain the wholeness of his being; and integrity means precisely to retain this wholeness. The inner-directed person develops only that part of himself which the ideal can compass, and that is always fragmentary.

An inner-directed man cannot appreciate and cannot understand the individuality of persons opposed to his ideal. He cannot even understand appreciatively the individuality of persons who share with him his own ideal because every unique individuality is always vastly more than any ideal; and the inner-directed person judges people in terms of their ideal and not in terms of their unique individuality in all its depth and fullness. Even when the ideal is to appreciate the unique individuality of every person, this appreciation must be created by the actual process of interchange which is always far more complex and diversified than any ideal can comprehend.

There is nothing wrong with ideals in their proper place. Everyone should have them. The question is not whether we should have ideals. The question is rather this: What is the organizing agency which creatively develops individuality in such a way as to have freedom? Is it ideals or is it the actual process of interchange with persons when this interchange creates appreciative understanding, mutual learning in depth and mutual enrichment?

Ideals must be cast off and outgrown as the individual develops from childhood to youth to maturity and on through the years. Therefore, something other than ideals must be the creative organizer of the developing personality. This something else is the creativity repeatedly set forth in this writing.

In contrast to the inner-directed person dominated by an ideal Riesman describes another kind of person whom he calls "other-directed." The other-directed person should not be confused with one undergoing creative transformation by way of interchange with others, here called creativity-directed. The other-directed man does not integrate what he gets from others into the unique individuality which is his true self. He does not learn in depth. Rather he superimposes upon himself the kind of character which will win the favor of those with whom he associates. This superimposed character suppresses and dwarfs his own individuality and does not allow it to develop. The other-directed person puts on the character which suits the occasion somewhat as one puts on a suit of clothes. This is a kind of socialization, but it is not individualism.

Over against both the inner-directed and the other-directed is the person dominated by a tradition. He will not interchange with others or accept anything from others beyond the bounds prescribed and imposed by his tradition. The tradition-directed and the other-directed do not exemplify individualism; the inner-directed and the creativity-directed do. But the inner-directed and the creativity-directed represent two opposing kinds of individualism. Only the second of these two kinds of individualism can be identified with freedom.

Obviously no human being is ever completely and perfectly any *one* of these four types we have mentioned--the inner-directed, the other-directed, the tradition-directed and the creativity-directed. Everyone is to some degree all four, although one of these types may dominate over the others in the case of certain individuals. The only purpose of considering them here is to bring out the kind of individualism which makes for freedom by setting it in contrast to other developments of the individual which are opposed to freedom. Individualism is all too frequently praised or condemned without making the proper distinctions. These distinctions are of utmost importance in dealing with the problem of freedom.

Important Distinctions

The ever closer weaving of the network of interdependence between individuals and peoples renders the individualism of the inner-directed increasingly frustrating to the individual and disruptive to the social order. Also, every ancient tradition is becoming increasingly diluted and merged with other traditions. This leaves widely open only two of the four ways of individual development, namely, the other-directed and the creativity-directed. Increasing social complexity is narrowing the opportunities and possibilities of life for the inner-directed and the tradition-directed while widening them for the other-directed and the creativity-directed. As the inner-directed and tradition-directed are crowded out, only the other two alternatives are open; and of these only the creativity-directed individualism brings freedom. The other-directed cannot have freedom when we understand freedom to be the bringing of the whole self into action by development of the unique individuality of each.

Freedom in our society has been long identified with individualism without distinguishing between the individualism confined by an ideal and the individualism released by creative interchange. Present social developments make this confusion increasingly dangerous. Our society cannot have the unity which gives power and protection nor the freedom which develops the constructive potentialities of the individual until the one kind of individualism is rejected as a goal of life and the other accepted.

To develop the constructive potentialities of one's own individuality, one must learn from others beyond the bounds of one's preestablished ideal. Otherwise there can be no creative transformation of the mind and no full development of those endowments which mark the human level of life. What the individual gets from others must undergo transformation as it is absorbed into her or his own unique self, analogous to the way chemicals are absorbed and transformed in the growing plant. But this learning from others and this appreciation of others must involve the whole self so far as possible and not merely the

- 31 -

idealized self of the inner-directed person or the consciously adapted front of the other-directed. If this learning from others does not creatively transform the self in the wholeness of its being so far as this is possible, the learning and the appreciation only transform the top layer of the conscious mind. The deeper layers are unchanged or developed in ways opposed to the conscious level. This split within the mind is opposed to freedom because the conscious level of the mind is frustrated and so held in bondage by the unconscious level. When it is not the whole self which learns but only a part of the self, the part which learns is obstructed and tricked by the part which does not. Thus learning from others often reduces the freedom of the individual. One becomes less able to make decisions wholeheartedly or to follow any course of action with one's whole self. Command of personal resources is lost. Much learning in school is of this sort. In this way "educated" people often have less freedom than the "uneducated."

Kinds of Interchange Opposed to Freedom

The social process includes many other kinds of interchange besides the one here distinguished as creative. At least five other ways of interacting can always be found where individuals are associated. These other ways reduce freedom to the measure that they prevail over creative interchange, while freedom is increased to the measure that these other ways are subordinated to creativity. Consequently the problem of freedom demands that we distinguish these other ways of acting on one another. If we do not distinguish them we cannot strive intelligently to make them subordinate to the creativity which magnifies freedom and individuality.

The kinds of interchange which are opposed to freedom can be briefly described. One is deceptive interchange in which the individual conceals from himself or herself and from others certain disagreeable things or fearful matters which he or she does not want to recognize and face up to. Another kind of interchange which is opposed to freedom is the manipulative. This is the use of propaganda or other brainwashing devices to mold other persons into tools, to control and dominate them and make them think and feel and do and be to serve the purposes of the manipulator. Thirdly, there is muddleheaded interchange in which a miscellany of trivialities are passed back and forth but are not integrated into a coherent whole and contribute little or nothing to the development of the individual. Then there is reiterative interchange in which one merely goes over the old routine. Since life requires a great deal of routine, reiterative interchange is necessary and may be used to produce conditions favorable for increase of freedom, but it may also do the opposite. By itself it does not make for freedom and may enslave one to rigid habits of thought, feeling and action. Lastly there is adaptive interchange in which the individual puts on a false front to meet the demands of changing situations and interpersonal relations. Obviously such adaptations cannot engage the whole self. This last kind of interchange characterizes the other-directed person.

Creative Interchange and Liberating Religion

Over against all these is creative interchange in which individuals express themselves truly and fully to one another; in which each welcomes and seeks to understand the undisguised individuality of the other; each gets the view held by the other and absorbs it into a personal view with whatever modifications this integration may require. In this way each expands and enriches the fullness of personal experience and increases the depth of reality which enters into personal consciousness.

This creative transformation of the individual is always reduced to small dimensions compared to what it might be. The obstructive processes of the other kinds of interchange above described are the obstacles to overcome. Freedom shrinks when creative interchange becomes a mere thread in the woven strands of these kinds of interchange which make up the rope of the total social process. Freedom grows when the creative strand becomes dominant over the others. The place of liberating religion in the struggle for freedom is to help individuals give sovereign place in their lives to the creativity which develops the individualism of freedom.

Nothing can be more productive of evil than religion and nothing more productive of good, depending on what it is to which individuals give themselves in religious faith. Nothing can enslave more abjectly than religion, and nothing can liberate more completely--hence the importance of liberating religion in the cause of freedom. Liberating religion in contrast to all other kinds has two outstanding features. It practices ultimate commitment to creative interchange, generally under some other name such as God, Christ or whatever; and it practices confession and repentance for any unfaithfulness to this commitment, thus preserving the integrity of individuals.

If freedom is to be saved and increased under conditions now prevailing, this kind of religion must be extended more widely among people. If only a few practice it, the other kinds of religion will create social conditions reducing freedom to a minimum despite what the few can do.

We must not be misled into thinking that the more diversity we have in religion the more freedom, when the diverse forms of religion enslave and do not liberate. There is only one kind of religion which can liberate and that is liberating religion. This is a tautology, but it must be emphasized because of the absurd notion so widely prevalent that diversity in forms of religion is a sign of freedom. There is only one kind of diversity which can be identified with freedom and that is the diversity which liberates the constructive potentialities of each unique individual. Every other kind of diversity is opposed to freedom or else irrelevant. Most diversity which we see in the world is not the expression of the constructive potentialities of unique individuals.

Since only one kind of religion liberates, the utmost diversity which grows with freedom must be sought by inducing all people to practice the same kind of religion and no other. The utmost diversity and freedom can be had only when all people do the same thing in one particular, namely, do what is required for the utmost diversity and freedom. If we are to have maximum liberating diversity, the same identical conditions must prevail everywhere when these conditions are necessary to sustain such diversity.

A further feature of the human society now emerging makes it imperative to distinguish between the two kinds of individualism, rejecting one and promoting the other. No civilization can survive in the days to come without a cohesive order tightening the bonds of control over individuals far beyond the kind of order which has prevailed in the United States and in the Western democracies generally for the last two hundred years, more or less. This is so for two reasons.

During the immediate (and perhaps long-term) future, there will be a terrific struggle for dominance between the Russian system of control and that of the Western democracies with the United States preeminent. It is to be hoped that neither side will entirely subordinate the other and that the two will in time develop some kind of universal order. But the Western world cannot hold its own in this struggle without tightening the bonds of unity and control far beyond what have prevailed among us in the past. This is so because the power of a people depends upon internal unity and control over all individuals and parts to the end of unified action. The problem of the West, then, is to have the most powerful cohesive order combined with utmost freedom for individuals. This cannot possibly be achieved with the individualism of the inner-directed but it can be with the individualism of the creativity-directed. The latter thrives on the closest bonds of unity because it is an individualism developed by interchange with others. This requires close bonds of unity while at the same time widening and deepening and strengthening these bonds continuously. Furthermore, the bond of unity developed in this way is not merely between individuals who can have personal acquaintance with one another. Even more powerful and indefinitely more comprehensive is the bond created by common devotion and religious commitment to this kind of interchange wherever and whenever it may occur. Millions of people can share this common devotion and religious commitment even when only a few of them may have interpersonal relations with one another. They who have deference toward the unique individuality of every other and who strive above all things to build and sustain institutions and social relations most favorable for this kind of interchange, will have a unity more powerful than any other and one which can grow continuously more wide, deep, and powerful and include millions in the fellowship of faith.

So far we have considered the need of social unity in order to survive and hold our own in the struggle for power and dominance now raging throughout the world. In time this competition for dominance must end in some kind of world-order if civilization is to survive. When a world order does develop, powerful social cohesion and control of all individual members will continue to be necessary for another reason. If diversity is not to be ironed out by a dictatorship imposing a world-order and if the increasing power of individuals and groups to wreck the world is to be directed to constructive ends and away from destructive ends, the minds and loyalties of people must be shaped and guided by a common devotion and religious commitment. This ruling devotion must continuously widen and deepen the sense of mutual concern for one another. It must bring to each the realization that the deepest roots of one's own individuality and the highest reach of one's constructive potentialities are fed and nourished by the kind of interchange commanding the ultimate commitment of all.

For these reasons the individualism arising out of creative interchange and devotion to it is the only kind which can sustain civilization in the future. This kind of individualism is the only kind which can give to each person the sense of belonging, the sense of being highly esteemed and cherished, combined with the highest development of the appreciations and powers uniquely possessed by each individual. This is the road to freedom and to power; to social order and to individual freedom; to control of the individual while releasing this person's constructive potentialities. But this road cannot be followed unless we distinguish between the two kinds of individualism, cleaving to the one and forsaking the other.

CHAPTER 4
The Selective Agency
of Pessimism

One well-known fact about life is that many forms become extinct because they cannot meet the changing demands of existence. They die out because they cannot undergo the kind of transformation required to sustain themselves under new conditions. This applies not only to the biological organism; it applies also to psychological and social organizations. Many kinds of social organization become extinct because they cannot be reorganized to resist the disintegration which sets in when problems demand solutions very different from the past. Many individuals are overwhelmed with anxiety, discouragement and despair when developments occur requiring a transformation in their way of life and in their attitude of mind. In this sense and in this way all forms of life from the simplest organisms to the most complex civilizations and human persons are subject to a selective agency which eliminates some while others continue. But no form of life can continue unless it undergoes the kind of transformation required to sustain itself under changed conditions.

Transformation for survival may take either one of two directions, with all gradations and variations between the two extremes. The change may be in the direction of increasing insensitivity and unresponsiveness behind some protective device. One example at the biological level is the development of a hard shell like the turtle; another is massive size like the dinosaur; another is the parasite. At the psychological level this direction of change appears in what are popularly called "defense mechanisms" of many kinds. By these devices the mind excludes from awareness the demands of changed conditions. One may construct illusions to conceal the need for reinterpretation of old loyalties, habits and affections. In some cases one may be acutely sensitive to external happenings but interpret them in a way to resist any change in certain cherished ideas about oneself or the world or society or God or anything upon which one has come to depend for a sense of security.

A further fact about the working of the mind should be recognized which may seem to contradict what has just been said but is not truly contradictory. The mind necessarily seeks stability and order in the world with which it deals. It does this by ignoring and selecting and interpreting what it finds until some order is achieved amid the chaos of impressions which pour in upon it. This is the way the mind always operates whether in science, common sense, religion, art, philosophy or in understanding the mind of another person.

Now this order which the mind constructs in interchange and cooperation with other minds not only excludes the irrelevant and inconsequential. It also excludes much to which the organism must respond in order to survive. It excludes much to which the organism must respond in order to sustain the conscious mind and enable it to operate at the level of the prevailing culture. Ideally all this excluded matter should be included in the order which the mind constructs; all advances in science, philosophy, art, religion and common sense moves in that direction. But due to human limitations much is always excluded to which response must still be made. This conflict between the stability of the order achieved to date in the mind and in society and these excluded responses is the cause of endless trouble in human life. Due to this conflict there is always a struggle to maintain order against the disruptive power of these excluded responses. This is true whether one thinks of the cosmic order which the mind has constructed or the social order, whether one thinks of the order which the mind seeks in the family or in business, whether one thinks of order in the sense of an understanding of the minds of one's associates or an understanding of the meaning and purpose of one's own existence. Always there is conflict between the order which the mind must have to be rational, intelligent, and purposive, and the disruptive and deranging demands of organic, unconscious, and conscious responses to matters which no achieved order can include.

When the individual is naive and unsophisticated and when the culture renders all humanity relatively naive, humans can find security in the order which the mind has constructed and in terms of which it interprets the goals of human existence, the being of God and the universe, the moral principles to guide conduct and the system of social organization which promises the greatest good. But in time humanity discovers that no order which the human mind can construct can be indefinitely maintained against the demand of changing conditions and the disruption of excluded responses. When this discovery emerges some may comfort themselves with the thought that even though no order which the human mind is able to conceive can comprehend and stabilize the whole of all which is and the tumultuous changes of time, nevertheless there is such an order eternal and all-inclusive. But this is a self-contradiction. An order which the human mind cannot conceive is no order at all relative to that mind. An order which is incomprehensible to the human mind is identical with chaos for that mind. The only kind of order which enables the mind to infer and predict, to achieve ends and pursue ideals, to guide action and understand other minds, is an order which the mind has achieved for itself. Any other order is disorder so far as concerns the operation of that mind.

Creative Transformation

When a civilization develops to the point where persons are able to reach this understanding of themselves pessimism begins to operate as a selective agent. It operates to eliminate those who can find no meaning, no purpose, no security apart from an ultimate and inclusive order adequate to all times and places and changes ever to occur. However, this selective agent saves, inspires and exalts those who find their ultimate security in following truth wherever it leads and undergoing creative transformation without conflict. Creative transformation of the mind results when creativity brings forth an order which includes more beauty, truth and love. More accurately stated, this expansion of the mind enables one to experience more richness of felt quality, more comprehensive reaches of inference, more profoundly appreciative understanding of other persons over the barriers of greater difference.

Creative transformation could not occur without conflict between the order achieved to date and responses not included in it. These excluded responses generate the innovating insights which lead to a more inclusive order provided the insight is tested and developed by the method which discovers error and distinguishes truth. But excluded responses conflicting with the achieved order cannot do this if the mind resists change and cannot tolerate the anxiety caused by confusion and uncertainty during the transition from the old order to the new. The mind will resist this kind of change and cannot tolerate the anxiety of confusion and uncertainty if the mind seeks and finds its ultimate security in some order whether it be achieved or ideal, whether it be its own order or be attributed to God.

- 41 -

One only has a mind most open to innovating insights generated by responses which conflict with every known order who seeks and finds one's security not in any order but in creativity itself. Here we have, perhaps, the most important issue in the conduct of human life.

"Is there no end to this kind of change?" is the querulous rejoinder. Everlasting change with only a possibility of improvement but no assurance and with no final order to point the way and provide ultimate security and meaning is intolerable. Thus speaks one kind of mind. Furthermore it may all end at last in the final obliteration of humankind. Thus speaks the person selected for extinction by the agency of pessimism. Thus speaks the civilization selected by the same agency for extinction.

What the pessimist says is altogether correct when she or he speaks about everlasting change with no final assurance of betterment and the possible obliteration of human life at the end of it all. The difference between the pessimist and the one selected for continued and confident living lies not in their understanding of the facts. The difference lies in where they find their security and that in turn depends on what commands their ultimate commitment. If they give themselves in the wholeness of their being to an order allegedly or desirably final, comprehensive and enduring, they become hopeless with loss of meaning for human living when the truth is discovered about humanity and its condition. But if they give themselves in the wholeness of their being to the power which creatively transforms when one commits oneself to it and when other required conditions are present, the meaning of life is not lost and hope and courage do not fail. Thus does the selective agency of pessimism operate in human life.

Changes in Language

These two ways of dealing with change in the basic order as conceived to date by the human mind can be illustrated by noting the two ways in which a language may change. Language, understood in this context to include all symbols whatsoever, is the supreme agency for dealing with everything in existence and everything in the abstract forms of possibility. It more than anything else makes possible the human mind and the human way of life. When conditions change in any radical manner either new words must be invented or new meaning given to old words in order to refer to these new conditions, to think about them, to analyze them, to distinguish cause and effect in relation to them, to develop inferences and imaginative experiments concerning them and make possible all the other mental operations with which the mind deals with its world.

Now this adaptive change in the language may not be creative. The new meanings attached to words may not extend the reach of human understanding, may not bring to consciousness a greater variety of felt qualities, may not permit more rigorously logical constructions of thought, may not enable individuals to enter into an appreciative understanding with a greater diversity of other minds or to discern in greater fullness the incomparable preciousness of the human person in self and others, or to exercise more power of control over happenings. The change in language might be in the opposite direction or, at best, merely maintain the same level as before. If the change in language diminishes the five dimensions of creative transformation just listed, we have what is properly called a decline of the civilization or culture in question. This decline may reduce the anxiety of those who find their security in final commitment to some established order or illusion about an order. But it is a change in the opposite direction from that of the creativity which creates, sustains, saves and progressively

- 43 -

transforms the human way of life. It is a change which diminishes instead of increasing the spiritual resources for human living.

Spiritual Resources

Spiritual in this context refers to resources in the form of the meaning attached to symbols. Spiritual development is development in that use of symbols which increases the five dimensions of creative transformation listed in the preceding paragraph. The abilities made possible by these spiritual resources include administrative ability and intelligent political action as well as artistic achievement and religious worship. They include scientific knowledge and scientific imagination as well as capacity for love and friendship. Resources not spiritual are machines and buildings, mines and forests, biological health and vitality and all other embodied forms of energy available for human control. Spiritual resources will ordinarily enable people to create material resources, but the two do not necessarily go together. A people may have abundant material resources without comparable spiritual resources when the material goods were produced by others of a previous generation or by people of a different culture from that of the people now in possession. Again a people may have magnificent spiritual resources with very little of the material. Some of the colonists who first came from England and Europe to this continent had great spiritual resources on arrival but the material goods in their possession were most meager.

With this understanding it is plain that the one thing which has lifted human life above that of the lower animals, the one thing which makes human life possible and failure of which drags us down toward extinction, is progressive accumulation of spiritual resources. What makes possible this accumulation beyond any known limit is the reconstruction of the basic and most comprehensive order achieved by the human mind at any one time. Therefore unfailing courage and hope and zest for living cannot be derived from commitment to any order achieved to date or any possible order ever to be achieved. Courage and zest for living at the human level can be had only by finding ultimate security in creative transformation itself. But this requires ultimate commitment to this creativity. Doubtless this creativity has its own order in the sense that it cannot occur unless required conditions are present. But order in this sense is very different from order in the sense we have been considering it.

The accumulation of spiritual resources in the sense indicated produces a more complex and numerous society of interdependent individuals and institutions. This increases complexity and accelerates social change. This makes more imperative and more frequent the reconstruction of any order in which individuals seek security. Thus the anxiety involved in such reconstruction is intensified for those who find security in achieved order and not in creativity. Everyone, even those who find their ultimate security in commitment to creative transformation, suffer more or less anxiety when change occurs in those assumptions and orders which sustain the way of life followed to date. Thus a kind of dialectic is generated which is a transition back and forth from an established order providing more or less security, then shifting to a reconstruction which intensifies anxiety, then shifting back to an order comprehending more complexity and change which therefore reduces security for those who depend upon it, followed by another time of reconstruction, etc. If this sequence and alternation continue, each new period of reconstruction must deal with a greater complexity and undergo more change. Therefore under the new conditions it is more difficult to achieve any comprehensive and sustaining order unless there has been an accumulation of spiritual resources adequate for this task. If there has been this accumulation, the new order is no more difficult to achieve than simpler ones relative to these added resources. If such accumulation has not occurred, the time comes when it is impossible to develop an order adequate to the complexities and changes of society and fit to meet the needs of the human mind living in such a time. When this happens either breakdown occurs in society and in the mind or else the dialectic is reversed and begins to move in the opposite direction toward simpler and more primitive conditions.

When moving in this opposite direction the transition is *from* an order suited to greater complexity and change to one suited to more simple conditions and less change. Here also occurs a dialectic swinging from times of intensified anxiety to times of relative security for those who depend upon commitment to an established order. But if this continues long enough, a time is generally reached when social groupings become so small and simple and isolated that some ancient way of life can take control of human existence. This ancient way is to live under the dominant control of a tradition which changes so slowly that no generation is aware of the change and all problems are simplified, although the impoverishment of spiritual resources may make them as difficult for the individuals concerned as those of a more complicated life. Under such conditions the same people for the most part live in the same group with the same associates from birth to death. All individuals thus associated have minds shaped and controlled by the same tradition and live together under the coercive regime of ancient custom and habit. Thus is the individual enfolded in an order which changes little and gives maximum security. Generally this downward movement of the dialectic stops at some such level; but if it does not, the human way of life becomes impossible. The sensitive and unprotected organism of humankind must either become extinct because not sufficiently protected by organizations fit for inference and control, or else the human organism gradually reverts to the subhuman. Presumably this second alternative cannot happen, in which case the extinction of humankind is the only result.

It seems from what we know about the history of past civilizations that the accumulation of spiritual resources has not kept pace with the increase in the complexity and the rate of change of social existence. In time this brings on either stagnation or reversal of the dialectic after the manner just described. It is the thesis of the present writing that this happens because the leaders at the high levels of complexity and change continue for the most part to seek security in some alleged order held to be comprehensive, final, eternal and changeless. Certainly this was true of Plato and Aristotle and their followers. It was true of the Stoics in Rome. It seems to have been true of almost all persons "of leading and light" at the high points of the civilizations of the world.

If our analysis is correct, it exposes the cause of the failure of nerve which happens at these high points. More accurately stated, it explains the inability to develop and maintain that sequence of orders necessary to carry civilization over the hump of increasing complexity. The creative potentialities adequate to this task cannot be released until large numbers of men and women, and especially those in places of supreme authority and responsibility, find the ultimate source of their security elsewhere than in any final order conceived or thought to be possible in history or beyond, in nature or the supernatural. The required capacity for undergoing creative transformation will not arise until a religion becomes prevalent which directs the ultimate commitment of persons to creativity. To date such a faith has appeared in individuals but has never become institutionalized and thus made sufficiently potent and prevalent to enable humankind to carry the upward dialectic very far. For this reason no people so far has been able to pass through that high divide which separates the first attempts at civilization which have occurred during the last six thousand years and that way of life beyond the divide. Beyond the divide is that way of life not yet achieved which sustains indefinitely the complexities and powers of advanced civilization along with the continued accumulation of spiritual resources beyond any known limit.

Advancing civilization increases the dependence of each upon a wider range of diverse individuals and organizations not only for success in commercial and professional projects but also for success in love and family, in friendship and self-respect, in social approval and prestige, in rearing children and keeping the peace, and in releasing the individual from the oppressive mechanisms of impersonal social control. The more diverse and numerous and rapidly changing are all the interdependent parts of the social system more difficult it is to maintain any order of mutual support unless there is proportional increase of spiritual resources. These are the difficulties and dangers and these are what cause the intensified anxiety and pessimism here called the selective agency in human life at the level of advanced civilization. Any attempt to allay this anxiety and pessimism can only be a palliative which does more harm than good unless it is done by religious commitment to the creativity which accumulates spiritual resources.

Here is the most acute problem confronting our civilization and the Western world. It can be stated thus: How to reduce the surge of pessimism and anxiety not by means of cherished illusion but with realistic appraisal of actual conditions and to do it not merely for cheer and comfort but to enable people to enter into that kind of interchange which accumulates spiritual resources for dealing constructively with the problems assailing us?

That question has its answer but the answer lies beyond the reach of politics and government, economics and industry, art and science, although these all must play their proper part. The answer must be found in religion, but not in every sort of religion. Only one kind of religion has the answer. If liberal religion can reach maturity before the hour of opportunity passes the affirmative answer will be ours.

With this understanding of the problem the next four chapters will be devoted to a study of what is involved in bringing liberal religion to maturity.

CHAPTER 5
Immature Liberalism

Maturity and immaturity are so related that each defines the other. Hence, a glance at immature forms of liberal religion is preliminary to a study of its maturity.

Religious liberalism is widely misunderstood and inadequately represented by its advocates. This is to be expected because it is in the making. What it might be when grown to full stature and power is not apparent from many forms which it has assumed. But critical expression of some of these immature expressions of liberal religion may help to reveal some of its possibilities. That is the purpose of the following criticisms. They are made in no unfriendly voice. Liberal religion more than any other kind is capable of self-criticism and self-correction. Hence, the purpose of this critical examination by one who professes to be an advocate of a transformed liberal religion.

The Goal of Liberal Religion

They who profess liberalism generally agree that the liberal must strive for togetherness in difference, for freedom of the individual combined with fellowship, for right to be oneself combined with vital participation in society. Perhaps these affirmations can be put into one statement by saying that the goal of liberal religion is to provide maximum freedom joined with fullest fellowship for each individual.

Freedom and fellowship for each individual is certainly

the goal of liberal religion. But no adequate goal is defined when we stop with this statement. Freedom and fellowship must be analyzed and interpreted and their relation to each other made plain before we know what the objective of liberal religion truly is. But even this is not enough. If liberal religion is to have constructive power to shape society and the course of history it must know what is the process of transformation which produces this union of freedom and fellowship for each individual. Also, it should know at least some of the more important conditions which must be present in order for this process of transformation to operate effectively. Finally liberal religion should develop and practice those rituals and ceremonies of public and private worship by which the whole person can put herself or himself under the dominant control of this transforming power.

Liberal religion can become an evil instead of a good when it fails to meet any of these requirements, namely, define its goal so that people can know just what is the objective for which everyone should strive throughout life, distinguish the process of transformation which produces what is sought when required conditions are present, specify some of the more important of these conditions and, finally, practice effectively the methods by which the whole self is continuously committed and rededicated to this transformation. Such commitment is what enables the individual to tolerate the anxiety experienced during the transition from an old to a more adequate order of life.

When all this is not done by liberal religion the individual breaking free from the constraints of tradition and other authorities may be in a worse state than before becoming a liberal swinging free. A liberal who has not done all this has what Erich Fromm calls "freedom from" but does not have "freedom to." Such a man knows the constraints which he wants to cast off but he does not have a ruling

- 51 -

devotion and sovereign purpose in common with others. Without these his constructive powers are not released nor his potentialities developed. In this state of "freedom from" without "freedom to," psychological compulsions develop which drive him to seek compensation for loss of fellowship and security at the deeper levels of his being. Fellowship and security can be had in the ancestral order which he has cast off. They can also be had in a fellowship of full commitment to creative transformation. But the liberal who has left the one and has not attained the other is at loose ends. Consequently he or she is subject to instability and the psychological compulsions to which the insecure are driven.

Twelve Inadequate Goals

Since these weaknesses and evils threaten the liberal it may be useful to examine some of the inadequate and misleading goals often proclaimed as distinguishing this form of faith. No attempt will be made to cover all the misleading directives set forth in the name of liberal religions but a dozen are selected as a sample of all the others. Each of these will be scrutinized briefly to show how it can lead astray if not defined and developed more fully than is ordinarily done when it is proclaimed.

(1) Diversity is often identified with freedom. But Hitlerite Germany had more diversity than the United States. No diversity in the United States was ever so great as that between the way of life of the leading Nazis and the inmates of the worst concentration camps; nor between the Gestapo and the hunted refugees; nor between all the different peoples and cultures from North Africa to the Ukraine brought together under Hitler at the height of his power.

The same great diversity can be found in Russia today.

The differences of thought and feeling among the various divisions in the United States are not as great as between the rulers of Russia and people who most bitterly resent their rule. Stalin rose to power by allowing the different peoples in the USSR to retain their diverse languages and cultures so long as they accepted his political control. Consequently, public pronouncements in Russia must be issued in many different languages to reach the people.

The point of all this is to show that diversity without further qualification does not provide freedom but may be the exact opposite. Diverse peoples and diverse minds cannot be free in association with one another unless they hold in common certain basic convictions and commitments which are liberating. Without this kind of uniformity or sameness prevailing no people can be free. Therefore, to proclaim diversity as the mark of a liberating religion is a mistake unless the statement is carefully qualified.

(2) Liberals often describe themselves as individuals who seek and welcome social change. But the greatest social changes in recent history have been produced by the Nazis and Communists. Surely they do not follow the high road to freedom and liberalism. To promote change without agreement on the kind of change which brings freedom and fellowship to the individual is highly dangerous. To go from life to death is just as truly change as to pass from death to life. Reversion to barbarism is social change as truly as the opposite.

(3) Often a distinctive mark of liberalism is said to be criticism freely directed at every purpose, belief and policy. But criticism without agreement on principles and methods for distinguishing true from false, right from wrong and better from worse can only lead to confusion and frustration ending either in stalemate or coercive domination of one side over the other. Liberal religion becomes another name for futility when criticism is rife without agreement

and union on the principles and methods of criticism.

(4) Liberalism is often identified with individualism. Two kinds of individualism have already been distinguished in chapter 3. Only one of these exemplifies creative freedom. The other can be the foe of liberalism. Hence the need for further qualification when liberal religion claims to be the champion of individualism.

(5) Non-conformity is sometimes set up as the mark of the liberal. But a large part of non-conformity is crime. Here again two kinds must be distinguished. A great deal of conformity is indispensable to provide the conditions and tools for progressive creation of the mind. Learning to read and write and speak correctly, obeying the law of the land, observing the rules of courtesy, and the list runs on. All these are necessary for the development of individuality. The highest and fullest development of individuality requires conformity with respect to all those matters which aid mutual learning and mutual understanding. There is a kind of conformity which does the opposite, but the two kinds should be distinguished whenever non-conformity is defended in the name of liberalism.

Non-conformity sometimes appears in the declaration that individual conscience is the only moral authority which the liberal can accept. But the psychology of personality presents massive evidence that the sense of right and wrong can be demonic. Local papers have recently told of a woman who beat a child put in her care until he died. She was a religious, conscientious person. She declared with apparent sincerity that she was not beating the child but the devil in the child. I myself have known parents who did horrible things to their children for conscience's sake. However, the conscience of some parents forbids them from disciplining their children enough to keep them from criminal careers.

(6) Striving for social improvement is said to distinguish

the liberal. But if liberals cannot agree and unite on the standard for judging what is improvement as over against the opposite, they are again reduced to futility and either strive against one another or do the wrong thing. Liberals like all others often disagree on what specific measures to promote and such disagreement with free discussion can be very constructive provided the disagreement is undergirded by some agreement on basic standards and ultimate commitment. But if these last are lacking there is no way to make discussion profitable and disagreement constructive in seeking social improvement.

(7) The right of each to think, speak and live as one chooses so long as one allows others the same right is another alleged distinction of the liberal. The best example of thinking, speaking and living as one chooses and allowing others the same right is found in the insane asylum among the non-violent, where each person is wrapped so completely and contentedly in his or her own illusions that he or she does not even perceive that others do not agree. Here again distinction must be made as in the case of the other alleged principles of liberalism. Allowing others to go their several ways so long as they allow you to go yours is not enough. No language, no culture and no human mind was ever created and sustained in that way.

(8) A society in which one has the right to make mistakes is another feature of liberalism. But making mistakes is of no benefit to anybody and is highly dangerous to everybody if the individual cannot learn from her or his mistakes. This cannot be done if there is no agreement on standards, objectives and commitment by which we distinguish what is a mistake from what is not. A mistake according to my standard may not be one according to yours. When you act rightly according to your standards but wrongly according to mine, you cannot learn from your mistakes because in your eyes they are not mistakes. In a highly

industrialized society where innumerable people have some control of forces which can do fearful damage, the individual has no right to make mistakes issuing in great disaster. The pilot of an airplane has no right to make the kind of mistake which plunges fifty people to their death. To be sure, mistakes of this kind will often be made, but they cannot be cherished as rights of the individual. This illustration, however, does not touch the most important issue. The consequence of some mistakes is not physical destruction but moral degradation. These will not so frequently occur if the same ultimate commitment and moral standard prevails generally throughout society. If this sameness does not prevail, blind and disastrous moral errors may multiply until civilization tears itself to pieces.

The individual should have the right to make mistakes but only after making the commitment and accepting the standards and objectives which enable one to judge one's own error and learn from one's mistakes. Also the individual's competence and devotion should determine the bounds within which he or she can make mistakes.

(9) A society which does not exclude anyone is sometimes said to be the goal of the liberal. If that means a society in which no one will ever be constrained or imprisoned to protect others, it is a futile dream. If it means that appreciative understanding of the unique individuality of the evil person is as urgent as like understanding of the good person, this statement about the goal of liberalism is profoundly true. The person in prison has as much claim to appreciative understanding as the person given largest liberties.

(10) Enhancement of life is another alleged goal of the liberal. But this suffers the same defect which has been reiterated. It seems to say something when in truth it is almost meaningless when further specification is lacking. Or, if you prefer, it has as many diverse and contradictory

meanings as there are individuals who use the words. Enhancement of life is one thing for the Communist, another for the Nazi, another for the lazy person who is a parasite, another for the everlasting go-getter, another for primitive people in contrast to the civilized and the list runs on. Enhancing life without agreement on what enhancement truly is can lead to conflict and futility.

(11) Truth, reason and freedom are said to be goals distinguishing the liberal. But truth and reason are tools, not ends. Also, we must know what is of primary importance about which to seek truth. There are truths to be discovered which enable one to prolong torture while keeping the victim alive and conscious and suffering to the point of insanity. Truth is a value-word which seems to suggest something grand and great. But truth, when we get it or approximate it, is knowledge; and knowledge can be trivial or important, superficial or profound, silly or wise.

The same indefiniteness applies to freedom. Unless freedom is otherwise interpreted, it refers to the state of being unconstrained and unconfined. This sets no goal and defines no objective. It is a state in which one might follow a ruling devotion, but until this devotion is defined and accepted freedom leads nowhere.

(12) Preciousness of persons has been called the distinctive objective of liberal religion. Certainly the preciousness of persons is a necessary evaluation for the kind of liberal religion here defended. But recognition of the preciousness of persons and their sacredness or holiness is an evaluation and not a guide or goal until we know what creates, sustains and develops the precious quality of persons. If liberals cannot agree and unite on this, they have nothing which distinguishes them from others, no matter how highly they evaluate persons each according to one's own standard and selection of what is precious in them. Perhaps persons are very precious to cannibals. It is said

that some primitive people eat the man or woman they most love and admire in order to acquire his or her virtues. Some people allegedly eat the flesh and blood of Jesus Christ because they adore him above all others.

Common understanding of the definitive characteristic of persons which makes them precious above all else may well give to liberal religion its unity, goal and driving power. But this outcome hangs on finding the correct answer to the question: What is it in human beings which makes each one incomparably precious beyond everything in the universe which is not a person?

Many proposed answers to this question cannot be accepted by any intelligent form of liberal religion, not only because such answers are false but also because they implicitly and unintentionally deny what truly is of such great value in each person. For example, it is often said that each person is most precious because God loves each with an infinite and unmerited love. But that is tantamount to denying any intrinsic preciousness in the person because the love bestowed is unmerited. Any religion adopting and living by such a doctrine cannot find what is truly lovable in fellow humans. All one can do with such a doctrine is to go through the motions of loving people because God loves them but not because they are lovable in themselves. Since we are not God, this attempt to love what is not lovable becomes a pretense. No wonder many people under guidance of this doctrine profess a love for human beings which their behavior plainly denies! To say that persons are precious because Christ died for them and not because of any quality in themselves is to perpetrate the same self-deceit in different words.

Again some say that what makes human beings precious are their immortal souls which can somehow be detached from psychosomatic individuals and taken to heaven--or to hell. But here again the preciousness is drained away from the actual psychosomatic individual with whom we deal in daily life. Also even the soul, if it can be justly subjected to eternal torment in hell, is shown by that fact not to be infinitely precious.

Sometimes it is said that what makes every person precious is the ideal possibility of what this person might become. But this is another way of concealing what is truly of supreme value in each person. I may glorify without limit the ideal possibility which I think hovers over every human individual. But we have already seen that no ideal can encompass the richness and fullness of the concrete individual. Also my ideal for the other person is never entirely correct in its judgment of what the other person ought to be and might be at her or his best. It contains all the bias of my own self-centered judgment and is more or less a strait-jacket imposed on the other. Consequently, the more devoted I am to my ideal for the other person, the more blind I am likely to become to what is most precious in this person's actual, present, concrete existence.

Still other answers to the question might be examined which are both false and treacherous because they conceal instead of expose the true worth of human beings. But the ones examined serve to show the need to set forth an answer nearer to the truth than any of these.

All the resources of inquiry now focussed upon personality seem to reveal that human beings are most precious because of the deepest and most imperative need wrought into their nature. This need is to love and be loved. More accurately stated, it is the need to appreciate and be appreciated in all the depth and fullness of the unique individuality of each. Nothing is more lovable than beings so completely made for love that they must destroy themselves if conditions will not permit them to love and be loved in all the depth and fullness of their nature. Humans are precisely these kinds of beings.

The malice and hate, the folly and treachery, the destructive and disgusting propensities in human beings arise because from infancy they have not been able to find that measure of love between each and other which human nature must have to develop. Hence, individuals resort to the vicious protective devices just mentioned. No matter how unconscious one may be of one's need to appreciate others and be appreciated by them, and no matter how hateful one's conduct and conscious thoughts resulting from inability to find this kind of interpersonal relation, the essential nature of the human being is still within. The ineradicable need is there, deep-buried as it may be. The turmoil and conflict and frustration, much of it kept below the level of consciousness, can be interpreted as a cry out of the depth for love. Such is the teaching of the psychology of personality as represented by Carl Rogers, Gardner Murphy and the Menninger Clinic, Erich Fromm, Karen Horney and Harry Stack Sullivan.

If one understands that the vindictiveness and fear, the evasiveness and indifference, the snobbery and exclusiveness, the cruelty and destructiveness, are "defense mechanisms" against a world which does not give the love which one must have to be his or her true and whole self, then one can see how precious every person truly is. "True and whole self" in this context means an organization of personality free of the inner conflict which breaks down the wholeness of the self. It is an organization of personality which experiences only that kind of conflict which results in progressive reorganization of the mind to more ample dimensions of appreciation and control.

This answer to the question, Why is every person most precious? is not complete or adequate. It is offered as a suggestion which might point the direction in which a mature liberal religion might move. In any case no verbal formulation of an answer to such a question can ever be

adequate. The right answer goes beyond every verbal formulation whatsoever. The right answer is a way of life and
an ultimate commitment.

CHAPTER 6
Mature Liberalism

Many different ideas of maturity are prevalent. It is futile to argue for one of these to the exclusion of the others. So long as common usage has not settled on one and only one meaning attached to a word, the several meanings must be accepted as correct no matter how irreconcilable they may be, since usage determines correctness. But to avoid confusion in this discussion one meaning only will be given to maturity. Also, I think it can be shown that some interpretations of maturity are concerned with matters much more important for human living than others.

Some Interpretations of Maturity

Maturity applies first of all not to religion or other expressions of the human mind but to the individual in her or his wholeness. Individuals are more or less mature. This maturity is expressed in different areas and the area which concerns us here is religion. In this sense we speak of liberal religion being more or less mature, meaning that individuals having a liberal religion can show more or less maturity in their liberalism. Also a fellowship of individuals sharing a common faith may display more or less maturity.

Since only the individual in his or her wholeness is more or less mature, religion being only one manifestation of it, maturity must first be defined in terms of the individual.

After getting our standard for judging levels of maturity by study of the person, we can apply it to religion as one expression of the person.

There is no final state of being which can be called maturity. Maturity is a progression. But levels of maturity can be distinguished. So we speak of attaining maturity in the sense of reaching a relatively high level in contrast to lower levels.

Prior to becoming adult, levels of maturity are connected with years lived, even when the individual does not reach the level expected at a given age. After becoming adult, one may continue to reach higher levels but these are no longer related to years lived. After physiological and neurological maturation is complete, increasing maturity takes on a different character. It then is determined by the way life is conducted and not by the time spent in conducting it. I shall try to show that progression toward higher levels of maturity after one becomes adult depends in great part on one's religion when religion is defined as commitment to the actuality which shapes the course of one's development.

For reasons stated we distinguish sharply between maturity in the sense of stages in developing an established organization of the personality prior to adulthood, and maturity in the sense of stages in development after the individual has attained a definite organization and established assumptions about things in general. We shall consider levels of maturity in this second sense only.

The Standard to Judge Maturity

The standard we shall use to judge maturity will have little if anything to do with intelligence and skill as these are often interpreted. Rather it will be the individual's capacity to undergo changes in basic assumptions when conflicts, difficulties and complications arise which cannot be brought under control without such change.

In one book, thirteen ranking psychologists devoted to the study of human personality describe experiments and observations which seem to demonstrate that the human mind always struggles to maintain or to recover a definite order in whatever is being experienced, no matter how much perception must select, ignore and interpret to achieve such an order.* Amidst all the happenings which occur, the mind struggles first of all to preserve stability in the comprehensive background against which objects are perceived. It also strives to achieve clarity of outline and definiteness of structure in objects perceived, although much of the total mass of data accessible to the senses must be ignored or excluded from the object to achieve this definiteness. Also, much interpretation must be added to the data themselves.

When innovations occur in the field of perception which threaten to disrupt the comprehensive order of the background and render the data of sense so confused and uncertain that no definite object can be distinguished, the mind struggles to overcome the confusion, driven by an anxiety which makes it difficult to endure the uncertainty. This struggle to restore an order enables the mind to anticipate outcomes and it can operate in either of two ways. In the first way, order may be restored by excluding from conscious recognition the disruptive happenings, thus retaining some order based on established assumptions of the mind. This produces the illusion of prediction and control, although the prediction and actual control of consequences becomes impossible when important new causative factors in the situation are ignored. The second manner of dealing with innovating and disruptive events is to tolerate the

---

* Blask and Ramsey, editors, *Perception: An Approach to Personality* (New York: Ronald Press Company, 1951).

uncertainty, confusion and anxiety long enough to enable creativity to change the established assumptions of the mind and bring forth a new order enabling the individual to predict and control the consequences of these strange happenings, to experience them richly and to understand and cooperate with other minds engaged also in dealing with the novel events.

This second of the two ways of dealing with disruptive and frustrating events is the way of maturity. It is the capacity to tolerate anxiety to the end of undergoing creative transformation. The first way of reacting to confusion and anxiety is the way of immaturity.

Of course, degrees of disruption and the amount of confusion, uncertainty and anxiety which one must endure, also enter into the picture. Maturity is measured by the amount of uncertainty and anxiety which the individual can endure long enough for creativity to generate the needed order or, if no order emerges, to endure indefinitely without imposing an old order which does not permit prediction, control, rich qualitative experience and understanding of other minds confronting like situations.

In Blake's and Ramsey's anthology, Carl Rogers defines perception as the organized meaning which we attach to stimulation of the senses. We learn to attach certain meanings to certain kinds of stimulation. These meanings are shaped partly to guide prediction and achieve control of consequences, partly to provide richness of felt quality, partly to enable us to understand and cooperate with others when these stimuli are encountered. By reason of this last, the organized meaning attached to certain stimulation of the senses in one culture may be very different in another society.

When new stimuli arise, ones which have not been experienced or have been ignored but which are now forced upon conscious awareness because they demand attention and action, we have the test of maturity. Can the individual endure the uncertainty, confusion and anxiety of not being able to attach any organized meaning to these new stimuli until a new meaning is generated (if ever) which provides for reliable prediction, control, richness of experience and understanding? If not, the individual fails to meet the test of maturity in this experience; if so, he or she shows maturity.

Maturity understood in these terms applies not only to stimuli emanating from material things. It also applies to that interpretation of internal stimuli which produces the idea one has of oneself. This belief about oneself is, of course, also shaped by what one thinks to be the opinion of others concerning oneself. No one is born with knowledge of the depth and fullness of the total being which is the self. No one ever acquires the whole truth about oneself. But some approximate this truth more than others. To approximate this truth, however, the first ideas one achieves about oneself in late adolescence, say, must be revised many times. One discovers developments in the self, hates and fears, vicious meanness and generous action, which threaten to break down one's assumptions concerning oneself. Can one tolerate the uncertainty about oneself until other assumptions have developed closer to the truth? And can one endure the anxiety of admitting evidence about oneself which undermines the self-esteem resting on the old assumptions? This anxiety may reach the dimensions of utter despair unless reduced either by some fond illusion about oneself or else by deeper commitment to the creativity which transforms the mind in a way to achieve a better understanding of oneself. The first of these two ways of reducing anxiety is the practice of immaturity; the second the practice of maturity.

Perhaps no anxiety is more distressing than this kind concerning the self. Therefore, one who can endure it until a more adequate idea of oneself emerges has met one of the severest tests of maturity. On that account it can be said that to know oneself with a minimum of illusion and error is a mark of advanced maturity.

This test of maturity also applies to the way one deals with the stimuli experienced when meeting unique individuals, each with facial expression, tones of voice, postures, gestures, statements and other stimulation calling for interpretation. The interpretation of these which one achieves is the understanding one has of the mind of the other person. If I persist in attaching the same meaning to all the diverse stimuli which come to me from unique individuals, I shall fail to achieve appreciative understanding of their unique individualities. To fail to do this indicates immaturity. To attain understanding of the unique individuality of others one must tolerate periods of uncertainty with that kind of commitment which enables creativity to produce the insight where understanding of the other person has been achieved to some degree. If one cannot or will not tolerate such periods, one will simply impose ready-made interpretations on the expressions of individuality, perhaps classifying people by some superficial characteristic, and then treating every one as though he or she were identical with the stereotyped picture of the class to which the person has been assigned. We all do this more or less, but the more mature one is, the less one does it.

This capacity to endure the anxiety involved in changing basic assumptions and undergoing creative transformation of the mind partly depends on heredity. Some organisms may have greater capacity for it than others. It certainly depends in part upon previous experiences from childhood on through life. But it also depends on how completely one is committed to creativity. If one seeks and finds security in giving oneself over to the keeping and control of creativity, one will be able to endure far more anxiety for

the sake of undergoing creative transformation of the mind
than one will be able to do if one seeks and finds security in
commitment to some established order with which the
mind operates along with the assumptions which sustain
that order. If unchanged order and unchanged assumptions
are the source of my security, I am lost when they can no
longer be sustained. But if my home is in creativity itself, I
can undergo great changes without despair.

Maturity in Religion

This brings us to the problem of maturity in religion. Since
maturity of the individual is measured by capacity to
undergo creative transformation of the mind, a person's
religion is more mature to the measure that it leads one to
give oneself most completely to the creativity which produces a sequence of periods of uncertainty and anxiety,
alternating with periods of newly attained assumption sustaining a more ample organization of the mind better fitted
to deal with the complexities and changes of human
existence. This alternation may continue indefinitely.

A religion fitted to enable one to pass through these
alternations is the religion of maturity. This form of religion is distinguished by certain characteristics, four of
which we shall examine.

A person's religion is more mature to the extent that the
person understands the problem underlying all other problems in the conduct of human living. For example, if I
think the chief problem of life and religion is to satisfy most
completely the desires I now have, I am less mature than if
I understand it to be that transformation of my present
desires which will yield more ample satisfaction. I become
still more mature when I discover that I can have a deep
and abiding satisfaction, mounting even at times to ecstasy,
if my whole life can be dominated and controlled by the one

supreme desire to undergo that transformation of mind which increases indefinitely the five dimensions previously noted--namely, knowledge, richness, community with others, mutual control, and discernment of the preciousness of persons.

To be ruled by this desire and to have this kind of religious commitment is maturity. Every other way of life leads to frustration and defeat. Only by this creative transformation of the mind can one discover what is better than anything one now knows, whether it be a better understanding of Christ or Nirvana or the Will of Allah or the mandate of heaven or the transcendent Being who rules the universe or whatever it be. Only by this creative transformation can the human being deal constructively with the increasing complexities and accelerated changes of advancing civilization. Only by this creativity is the human way of life distinguished from that of the lower animals. Only in this way can the sensitive and unprotected organism of humankind survive. This is maturity because it is based upon a better understanding of human nature and the destiny of humanity than other forms of religion.

If I think the chief concern of religion is to get my soul to heaven, my religion is immature because here again is a misunderstanding of the nature of human beings and the kind of life which our nature demands. Illustrations might be multiplied but the ones mentioned reveal the principle for judging the maturity or immaturity of any form of religion in respect to this first feature. In respect to this point, that religion is most mature which most correctly and comprehensively understands the nature of human beings and in consequence understands the problem which underlies all others in the conduct of human life.

The second mark of maturity has to do with distinguishing true and false beliefs. That religion is most mature which best understands and most effectively applies the method for doing this. The problem of knowledge in general and of religious knowledge in particular is enormously complex and controversial. It is impossible to deal with it with any fullness in the space permitted. Therefore we shall limit ourselves to examination of one point only which is selected because it seems to be the issue on which liberals have most frequently been misled. Liberals are not inclined to accept dogmatic authority, so that is not a form of immaturity which need concern us here. But liberals have turned to individual religious experience as the alternative to dogmatic authority. I shall try to show that this appeal to religious experience is a mistake unless carefully qualified.

An Example of Religious Experience

For purpose of this criticism let us take an example of religious experience which may seem fantastic but which embodies all the principles revealing the error of depending on religious experience to validate religious belief.

Suppose I believe this house to be an elephant and hold the belief with religious conviction. If I do, I shall experience this house to be an elephant because the belief will produce this experience. Also, the experience will then validate the belief. I first believe; the belief causes me to have the experience; I then point to the experience to show that the belief is true. I might take any other object to illustrate this procedure, such as a person believed to be God or the universe believed to manifest its Creator or the developments of history giving me the experience of a transcendent Being directing events to a final consummation. If I hold the belief with enough conviction, it will cause me to have the required experience; and the "religious experience" will then authenticate the belief. The same principles apply to the house-elephant experience as to the more common forms of religious experience just mentioned. But these principles can be examined more readily in a simplified form of experience, hence the use of the example of the house believed to be an elephant.

If this belief that the house is an elephant has been firmly established in my mind by what I believe to be a "divine encounter" with the house, and if the belief is supported by a devoted fellowship of believers who join me in worshipping the alleged elephant, and the belief is further sustained by an ancient tradition and powerful institution, if martyrs have died for the belief and if my fellow believers are all united with me in struggling against a powerful enemy who repudiates the belief, then I may continue to my dying day believing that this house is an elephant, especially if my soul's salvation is supposed to depend on holding fast to this belief. Furthermore, I can confirm the belief by appeal to religious experience, both my own personal experience and the universal religious experience of all who live by the same assumption, namely, that the house is an elephant. This I can do because precisely this assumption generates the experience.

I can hold this belief and have this religious experience while at the same time granting that the object is a house when approached by the secular mind. So likewise the person believed to be God is also a man or woman, the universe believed to manifest the power and glory of its Creator can also be experienced as "a collection of atoms," and the events of history revealing to faith a transcendent Being controlling the outcome can also be experienced as having no direction or goal. I myself can experience these matters in the secular way, but when I approach them in faith I have the religious experience which testifies to divinity in each case.

But now suppose I apply to the house-elephant that

method of inquiry which is able to discover and correct its own errors and illusions. I do this by developing the implications of my belief that the house is an elephant. If it is truly an elephant, I should be able to trace the route of its transportation to this place and the agencies which did the transporting. I develop the further implications of my belief by recognizing that elephants must eat. Therefore, if this is an elephant I should be able to discover the source of its nourishment, the farmers who produce it, the purchase price and much else. So I might continue to develop an intricate and far-reaching system of statements all implied by the belief that the house is an elephant. These statements must specify what can be observed at certain strategic points if my experience is truly that of an elephant; and the inability to observe these matters under specified conditions is evidence that it is not an elephant. If I follow this method I shall probably discover that the house is not an elephant.

There is one condition under which this method of inquiry is irrelevant. If the elephant-experience is a supernatural revelation or a divine encounter with a Being entirely different from all beings found in the temporal world, then the method of inquiry just described cannot be applied. It cannot because a non-temporal Being permits no predictions concerning what might be discovered in the course of temporal events such as traces of transportation, food-supply and anything else by which we test the truth of beliefs about happenings in the temporal world and beings which reside in time and space.

But if this method for finding what is true and what is false about the house-elephant experience cannot be applied, one must ask: How can one distinguish true and false beliefs in such cases? Many liberals have replied by saying that we know what is true and what is false by experience, meaning religious experience of the sort just described. But surely it is obvious that an experience provides no evidence for the truth of a belief when the experience is caused by the belief itself. All error and illusion arise out of experiences caused by holding a mistaken belief. One may appeal to dogmatic authority or to the psychological and social benefits allegedly derived from the belief. But error can be supported in this way as well as truth and there is no way to discover the error when one depends upon dogmatism or upon the psychological and social benefits of an illusion.

Beliefs held on such grounds that it is impossible to distinguish which are true and which are false are beliefs which can never be disproved. Beliefs so held are impregnable and cannot be shaken by any sort of inquiry. They who accept the assumptions of such a faith are immune to every challenge and every test. But they who do this should be honest about it and not conceal what they are doing. They can believe with conviction untouched by any kind of inquiry, but they have no knowledge whatsoever if knowledge means belief confirmed by evidence. They cannot distinguish between what is true and what is false in their beliefs, but that does not prevent them from believing with conviction unto death.

Whether or not the ruling beliefs of religion should be independent of the tests of insight, implication, prediction and observation as above described will be decided one way or another according to what one thinks is the basic problem which religion should solve.

The Basic Problem for Religion

Suppose the basic problem for religion is this: What is human nature and what does it require to be saved from self-destruction and transformed as human beings cannot transform themselves into the best which human life can ever attain? If this is the central problem for religion, there is no possible way to deal with it except by the method of inquiry which distinguishes true from false beliefs. If this problem is accepted as the chief concern of religion, resort to religious beliefs beyond the tests of insight, implication, prediction and observation is immature. One form of this immaturity is that reliance on religious experience which we have been criticizing.

We have examined two of the features which distinguish a mature form of liberal religion from immaturity. We have tried to show that one feature of a mature liberal religion is a correct understanding of the question which religion should try to answer; the other a correct understanding of the method of inquiry enabling one to find the answer.

Two other features distinguish a mature liberal religion but they must be postponed to later chapters. They are: (1) One's religion is more or less mature depending on how fully one understands what power is and what is the proper religious use of power. This will be studied in the next chapter. (2) One's religion is more or less mature depending on one's capacity to bring one's religion into close conjunction and cooperation with education and the school, with scientific research and industry, with government and family and all secular activities and institutions which can serve the ultimate commitment of humankind. This will be developed in the last chapter.

Two other features of a mature liberal religion will not be studied but must be mentioned. One concerns the relation of a mature liberalism to tradition. Mature liberals will appreciate, appropriate and use more of their tradition than conservatives because they are freer to examine and find value in all branches and aspects of it. For example, the outstanding achievement of our Western tradition is the enormous development of the sciences and the scientific attitude in dealing with all manner of problems. Liberals will appropriate this part of our tradition for their religion as freely and fully as any other part of our rich heritage.

A further feature of a mature liberal religion is its recognition and appreciation of mystery. Mature liberals will recognize and appreciate more profoundly than is possible in any other form of religion the depth and darkness of the mystery which encompasses life. This they can do because, unlike other religious people, they deny that any divine revelation or any claim of faith can penetrate this mystery. We know nothing save what can be discovered by the method of inquiry previously described, say the liberals. This lops off vast claims held by other forms of religion to penetrate this mystery.

Mature religious liberals recognize the large place which myth has in human life. For one thing myth makes us aware of the mystery just mentioned. But liberals deny that any myth can convey any truth to the human mind until it is translated into a proposition which states this truth and meets the tests distinguishing truth from error.

In discussing the several features of maturity its relation to freedom should not be missed. One is free to the measure that one can undergo inner changes in a way to master innovations otherwise disruptive and frustrative. This measure of freedom, we have seen, is also the measure of maturity. To the measure that one cannot undergo these inner changes due to internal resistances, one is not free to overcome difficulties, solve problems and gain needed insights. The measure of the degree to which we lack freedom is also the measure of our immaturity, according to the account of this chapter.

CHAPTER 7
The Problem of Power

Power in the sense here intended is the capacity to induce or require action by others in certain areas and forms. The area and form of action induced by an industrial executive is action to produce and market goods. So likewise government, home, school, church and other institutions have their respective areas and forms of action induced by the authority of those holding official positions. Power is the action of many people working together under the control of some agency which induces or commands it.

In some cases the agency of control is an institution and the source of command is the individual or individuals vested with authority by the institution. Power is also exercised by those having great wealth. They may or may not operate through institutional channels but in any case they induce action performed by many people, partly due to the prestige derived from wealth, partly due to payment for action and partly due to the expectation of other rewards which great wealth can bestow. Also outside institutional channels, as well as within them, the action of many people is induced by special individuals possessing endowments of personality and specialized training. Also the prestige acquired by some spectacular achievement may enable certain persons to make friends and influence people, which is another way of describing power.

Besides action induced by authority of institutions, wealth, personal endowment, special training, skill and spectacular performance, there is another source of power which has been rapidly declining in the Western world. Yet throughout human history the mightiest power over the minds and wills of the multitude has been exercised in this way. Its decline exposes the problem of power in our society. This source of power often operated through institutional channels but not necessarily. It was the power of a very few people having the aura of majesty and sanctity to command the multitude even to the point of utmost sacrifice, and without the need to explain the reason why.

In all ages and among almost all peoples excepting recent Western society a few persons had privileges traditionally established which the masses did not have. They had leisure, did no manual work, could wear ostentatious clothing permitted to no others and develop manners and qualities of mind which set them apart from the common people. Added to this was an ancient tradition, all-dominant and deeply wrought into the sentiments of all, which made everyone view these privileged few as a different kind of being from the rest of humanity. The privileged few looked upon themselves in this way as did everyone else. Consequently an individual reared from infancy as a member of this superior class acquired the habit of command and the air of unquestioned authority. The ordinary mortal would not think of refusing obedience to such a one except under very unusual circumstances. This ruling group, whether religious or political or both, could induce massive concerted action from all the people.

Evils of Power

Obviously great evils can accompany power exercised in this way. The needs and interests of the common people could not even be expressed in any adequate manner, much less considered. However, the rulers could not exercise power if they did not provide for the needs of the common people as they cared for the cattle and the dogs because the power of the few was nothing else than the concerted action of the many under their command. If the common people lacked health, vitality, courage and sufficient understanding to operate effectively, the power of the ruling few was reduced. Some rulers made the mistake of not caring for the people sufficiently to uphold their own power and were conquered by rulers who did. Thus to retain and magnify their power rulers had to care for the common people not because the people had rights, but because they were indispensable. Of course this is only one feature in the complexity of conflicts arising from the struggle for power and wealth, but it is one which concerns us just now.

This kind of power with all its evils did serve to uphold social order and direct social action. Perhaps without it civilization could never have arisen in the first place nor have been upheld during the thousand and more years when human beings were first learning to live in a complex society. Also while rulers may be just and benevolent and even democratic in intent, it is as true today as it ever was that government must be able to command the resources and concerted action of the people. If any particular government is unable to do this it cannot preserve public order nor secure its people against the aggression of governments having this power. Therefore care of the people must be of such kind as to give power to those in command. Any people sacrificing the power of their leaders for the sake of democracy will lose their democracy to other people who give greater power to those in control. This is the inescapable problem of power for the democracies.

Lippmann's Analysis

This problem has been examined by many. One outstanding writer on the subject was A. L. Schumpter in *Fascism, Socialism and Democracy*. But the most masterly treatment of it has been made by Walter Lippmann in his book *The Public Philosophy*. Lippmann's thoughts on the dangers threatening democracy have already been discussed in chapter 1. On the problem of power under democratic control he has much to offer and so we shall look further into what he has to say. On the subject of power Lippmann gives answer to the following question: How can the massive concerted action of the people in a democracy be commanded by the government to promote the security and well-being of the social system as a whole when the government is subject to local, partisan, competing and private interests and uninformed popular slogans?

No matter how high their intelligence, the minds of the people are rightly dominated by interests which concern them directly and for which they are personally responsible. These interests are local and private and concern organizations which form only parts, and generally competing parts, of the entire social order. But the executive branch of the government is responsible for the security and well-being of the entire society. Yet, says Lippmann, government in our democracy today cannot act in service of the public interests with the wisdom and power available to it because it is subject to the demands of private interests. Quite apart from any evil intent or selfish purpose, these competing private interests, precisely because they do compete within the social system, cannot be identical with the needs of that social system. People outside the executive branch of the government have neither the time nor the information nor perspective nor responsibility to understand problems world-wide in scope and subtly complicated.

We have our checks and balances and the executive

branch has a degree of independence. Also many matters are decided in cabinet and commissions, by experts and administrative agencies. Nevertheless Lippmann makes it plain that our government does not have the independence and power of command which any government must have to use the wisdom and control the resources available to it. Only the executive is in a position to understand and act intelligently on many matters vital to the common good and sometimes necessary to the survival of the democratic way of life. Over against the executive are the representatives of the people. They serve the interests expressed and promoted by organized groups and these are private and local. It is the duty of the representatives to serve these interests but on that very account they cannot have the perspective and responsibility fitting them to act wisely and independently of local interests in service to an order which underlies and comprehends all these diverse and transitory interests.

The people who benefit from democratic government, says Lippmann, no longer understand and accept the principles which sustain democracy. Furthermore, they are anxious and lonely because they have no communion with one another in sharing common convictions concerning what commands the ultimate allegiance of men and women and what should be the direction of human striving. Therefore, they have no shared allegiance which can unite them in defending and upholding democracy. Ultimate allegiance is left to the interpretations of private judgment so that no ruling devotion can unite the adherents of democracy. This is a fatal weakness, says Lippmann. Under such conditions the democracies cannot hold their own against social systems upheld by a dedicated elite who are united by shared convictions concerning what should be the goal of all human living and who are committed to it above all private interests, regardless of the error and evil of these convictions.

Few are better informed than Lippmann concerning what is actually going on in the world; few are more deeply concerned for freedom and few have shown more profound insight into social issues in books and other public statements running through many years of comment with world-wide observation and personal contact with those in positions of highest responsibility. If anyone has had opportunity to find out what is wrong with us, it is Lippmann. Of course that does not make him infallible. He may be mistaken but it is folly to thrust his ideas aside without serious consideration.

The key thought in his treatment of the problem of power in a free society is stated in the following quotation about the two functions of government. These two functions are, he says,

> *governing,* that is the administration of the laws and the initiative in legislating, and *representing,* the living persons who are governed, who must pay, who must work, who must fight and it may be, die for the acts of the government. I attribute the democratic disaster of the twentieth century to a derangement of these primary functions.
>
> The power of the executive has become enfeebled, often to the verge of impotence, by the pressures of the representative assembly and of mass opinions. This derangement of the governing power has forced the democratic states to commit disastrous and, it could be, fatal mistakes. It has also transformed the assemblies in most, perhaps not in all, democratic states from the defenders of local and personal rights into boss-ridden oligarchies, threatening the security, the solvency, and the liberties of the state.[*]

---

[*] Walter Lippmann, *The Public Philosophy* (Boston: Little Brown and Company, 1953), pp. 54-55.

What is the cause of this derangement of the two functions, one to govern, the other to represent? What has given such dominance to the function of representing that the other function, namely, governing, has become enfeebled to the verge of impotence? Lippmann replies to this question. He says it is caused first of all by the enormous increase in taxes and other sacrifices which the government had to demand of the people since the first world war. Since the representatives of the people must grant such demands and the people must be persuaded to approve, the government was placed in the predicament of submitting the course of public action to the judgment of the people. This inability of the government to make major decisions without popular approval results in subordinating the informed and responsible judgment of the government to the uninformed, slogan-ridden, diverse and competing interests of the multitude. These interests in turn find most effective expression in organized groups formed to promote special interests.

A further cause of weakness in democratic government should be noted. Persons in high position are elected and must win votes and retain popular favor by appealing to popular interests. But the minds of the electorate, as previously stated, are rightfully devoted to local and private problems and not to the top problems with which the government must deal. Therefore those most devoted to the top problems of the common good and the public interest are unfitted to win votes and retain popular favor because these must be won by appeal to what happens to possess the minds of the people at the time. This gives political advantage to leaders who serve special interests in opposition to the common good and who whip up hates and fears most appealing at the moment.

Problems in service of the public interest become increasingly world-wide and concern developments extending through long periods of time. However, the minds of the people become increasingly absorbed with local and private and transitory interests because democracy requires them to assume responsibility for these. But this unfits their minds for dealing with world-wide, inclusive problems concerned with long stretches of history. In face of all this the government in the democracies is forced to submit its problems to the decision of the people. Out of this arises the weakness of the democracies which will be fatal if not corrected.

The democracies have ample resources for resisting and turning back the massive repudiation of freedom which seems to be sweeping the world. But they cannot use these resources in the struggle against the foes of freedom until the government gains sufficient independence to exercise the knowledge and wisdom available to it.

This problem to be solved by the democracies might be viewed as that of avoiding the two horns of a dilemma. One horn is to avoid that weakening of the government which results when executive decisions are in bondage to the local, conflicting and uninformed interests of the people. The other horn is to avoid that ignoring of these interests of the people which results when executive decisions are not in bondage to the judgments of the people.

Private interests are precious because they express the needs of localities, groups and individuals which are truly different from one another. These must be expressed and satisfied so far as possible. But these diverse and changing demands must not be allowed to obstruct the action required to defend and strengthen what sustains them. Zeal for the golden eggs must not kill the goose that lays them. The struggle of each unique individual, each unique locality, each unique business organization or other organized group to get the special kind of golden egg it needs or wants will kill the goose, unless some agency cares for the goose. The unsolved problem of the democracies is to untie the hands of government at the top level so that they can care for the goose.

Democracy and freedom cannot be saved unless we can restore to democratic government the power to govern. This can be done, suggests Lippmann, by establishing again the idea of natural law and devotion to it. This idea and this devotion formed the basis on which the democracies were reared. But many things have conspired to dethrone this idea of natural law so that it no longer is accepted with the reverence and allegiance which once gave authority to the government when acting in its service.

Lippmann's diagnosis of our malady seems altogether convincing. His proposal for its cure does not. He himself casts much doubt upon the possibility of restoring reverence for natural law. But, as he himself admits, "natural law" has many meanings. If by its restoration he means belief in natural law as conceived by the Greeks, by the Roman Stoics and jurists and by the late Middle Ages, there is much reason to think it cannot be done. But if natural law can be interpreted to mean the conditions required for the operation of that process which creates the human mind and the human way of life and all the highest good of human life, then the suggestion takes on plausibility. But the laws of this creativity cannot be identified with any final ideal order after which all must strive. These laws or required conditions of creativity change as the human mind develops and society becomes more complex. Also these laws must be discovered and demonstrated by studying the way this creativity works under different conditions, thus finding those conditions under which it operates most effectively. In fact this is being done in the study of the developing mind of the child and what this development required; in the experimental study of methods of education, in the study of the problems of business management and many other like investigations.

Whether or not Lippmann would accept these demands of creativity and creative interchange as natural law I do not know. But in any case, his diagnosis seems sound and his proposed cure is also correct in so far as it is the claim that democracy and freedom can be saved only by restoring a publicly shared conviction and unifying allegiance which take priority over private interests. The only questions at issue are: What conviction, and allegiance to what? One answer to these questions has been set forth throughout this writing.

Lippmann says our salvation must be accomplished by a philosophy; but no philosophy can accomplish what is needed unless "philosophy" is understood to include commitment which takes priority over local and private interests. No philosophy can do this unless rituals, ceremonies and assemblies are practiced which cultivate, deepen and spread this commitment. Lippmann seems to recognize this, but uses the word "philosophy" and not "religion" for another reason and in this case perhaps with justification. Religion is identified with beliefs not subject to the tests of reason. But no allegiance can command the devotion of the people in our democracies unless its importance and rightful priority over other interests can be rationally demonstrated. No presentation of the common good in form of myth and symbol subject to devious interpretations can do what is required unless those myths and symbols can be translated into definite propositions subject to testing by the method previously described. Certainly myths and symbols will be used, but only to present with powerful appeal what is demonstrably true.

Saving Democracy and Freedom

If democracy and freedom are to be saved these are the two requirements: Demonstrable truth concerning the common good which underlies and sustains the diversity of local and private interests but not identical with any part or whole of them; secondly, a form of religion which leads people to trust and commit themselves to the common good sufficiently to allow their government to command resources and concerted action in its service independently of local and private interests. Also this devotion of religious commitment must control the leaders as well as the people and control those who exercise the power of authority in high positions of government.

Demonstrable truth and religious commitment combined in the manner stated is a mature liberal religion. It will not guarantee that executives in positions of responsibility will serve the common good. Partly because of their fallibility and partly because of their corruption they may often fail. But perfection is not here under consideration. A people more or less united by a truth and a faith which is not only cultivated by a form of institutional religion but is also the chief aim of education and is demanded by the prevailing form of industry will exert powerful influence upon all persons in positions of responsibility. The relationship of industry and education to this form of religion will be discussed in the next chapter.

The liberal religion now prevailing does not have the maturity required for this undertaking. It does not because it follows the popular liberalism of the day which identifies the common good with some approximate harmony of the conscious interests of individuals and organizations brought to expression in the form of a majority vote. Such harmonies, adjustments and compromises must be sought and must be expressed by voting with majorities determining the decision. These have their large and important place in every democracy. But all this must not be confused with something else. The something else is the demand of the creativity of interchange running continuously through many generations and is not to be interpreted in terms of the competing interests and the popular vote and the needs of the passing day.

No individual or group of individuals should be allowed to exercise the power of the executive without the consent of the people. But the consent of the people must be shaped by a religious commitment which enables them to judge with some wisdom who is fitted to govern. Also this religious commitment must be of such sort that the people can allow their chosen leaders to act and to command with the vision available to them. Finally and most important the demonstrable truth concerning the common good must reveal to the rulers that their own power and privilege reside in faithfully serving the creative interchange in every institution and in the lives of all the people.

At the beginning of the discussion of this chapter we noted that the old-time rulers, when intelligent, served the people for the sake of their own power and privilege because these were derived from the services of the people. To this end they cared for the people as they cared for their cattle. In the long run no government will faithfully serve the good of all the people unless they who govern can do it in a way to magnify their own power and privilege. In ancient times the power and privilege of rulers could be upheld by treating the people like cattle because power and wealth in those days came directly from the soil and the people living as serfs could raise crops and animals as well as, if not better than, educated people so long as no scientific knowledge was available for doing it. But today power and wealth do not come directly from the soil but very indirectly. Products of the soil must pass through intricate processes of transformation by an elaborate technology which the people must operate. Also elaborate scientific knowledge is available for raising crops. Consequently people cannot operate our elaborate scientific technology without a high degree of education and access to cultural privileges of many kinds. Also the machines cannot produce great wealth and power for the few unless the products of these machines can be purchased by the people and thereby pay for the investment in them. For these reasons any government today, to retain and increase the wealth and power of the few, must at the same time increase the wealth and power of the many. Therefore no elite and no government can increase the wealth and exercise maximum power in our civilization without shaping social policy in a way to magnify throughout the society the creativity which produces the minds and the initiative required to master scientific knowledge and the appreciative understanding of associated workers.

Demonstration of this truth will reveal to those who exercise greatest power in government that their own power depends upon magnifying the power, privilege and wealth of every one, provided all can be induced to work together for the public interest when public interest is understood to sustain and magnify the power and freedom of each. Management in industry is beginning to operate precisely in this way.

Religion's Exercise of Power

So far we have looked at the problem of power in its bearing upon democracy and freedom and have indicated the part which a mature liberal religion must play in saving democracy and freedom from the danger now threatening. Let us now look at the way such a religion should exercise power if it is to do its saving work in this time of democracy's peril. Perhaps this question can best be approached by a series of negations.

The power of a mature liberal religion does not reside in the church although the church has indispensable work to do. The power of a mature religion is not the ability of the church to induce or require concerted action of the people. Neither is it the ability of the clergy to move the people to action. Neither is it the power of sacrament and ceremony, nor power in doing any kind of institutional religious work. The church and the clergy might well cooperate to induce action of all the people but only in conjunction with the other major institutions; and the concerted action would be directed primarily not to service of the church nor to the practice of any kind of religious ceremony. It would be directed to constructive action in government, industry, school, family, science, art, the professions and in all the secular pursuits of life. The part of the church and its officials would be to deepen personal and group commitment to the common good which is served in all these different ways. The power of action resulting from this commitment would be the power of a mature religion pervading society and the lives of the people in all they do. It would not be centered in the church any more than in family, school, government, business, and other areas of constructive action.

The power of mature liberal religion operating in this way is impossible without close cooperation between church and school. This does not mean any institutional control exercised by the church over the school but it does mean that the whole system of education will be directed to searching the character of the common good and what it demands and instructing people from childhood onward concerning it. Without a system of education dominated by this aim there cannot be sufficient understanding of the commitment which the church seeks to deepen and improve. The great weakness of religion in our time springs from this lack of persistent, organized, intellectual inquiry into the character of what should command ultimate commitment. Institutional religion is almost entirely occupied with proclaiming some traditional answer to this question about what commands ultimate commitment instead of seeking a better understanding and deeper insight than popular slogans and symbols are able to impart.

Institutional religion cannot assume responsibility for this kind of inquiry and instruction needed to inform the minds of all concerning these religious problems. Such work lies outside the province of the church generally speaking. Such work must be done by the school and especially by the colleges and universities. But at present it is not being done. Until it is done the church cannot do its own work effectively, because the work of the church is to cultivate commitment to a reality which the people must first understand before they can give their devotion to it.

This connection between a mature liberal religion and education will be the theme of the next chapter.

CHAPTER 8
Liberal Religion
and Education

In a highly industrialized society the content and goal of education is determined by the demands of industry. This is true whether we like it or not. This does not mean that people who dominate industry dictate to the schools what they shall teach. Such domination of education by the arbitrary will of individuals should not be tolerated and is not the meaning of the claim just made. Rather, the meaning is this: when society is highly industrialized the social order will break down if it does not have the continuous and powerful support of industry; when industry takes the form of automation it will break down if it does not have the continuous and powerful support of education. Therefore, the primary concern of education to meet the needs of industry becomes a social necessity. It is not due to the machinations of powerful industrialists or of any other individuals. Under such conditions the domination of education by the needs of industry becomes an essential part of the culture without which the social system disintegrates.

The claim that automation will come is scarcely a prediction. It is already established in a number of places and is rapidly advancing into others. It is bound to take over the major industries although many small businesses will continue to operate in all the diversified ways they have always followed. Automation requires the kind of education which releases the powers of insight, imagination, communication and logical coherence in dealing with new problems never encountered before. This creativity will be needed not merely to initiate automation but continuously in its operation.[*] Education developing the mind in this way calls for the creativity found in the kind of interchange which has been described. Commitment to this creativity is what a mature liberal religion cultivates and deepens. This reveals the responsibility and opportunity for this form of religion in the age we are now entering.

Education and Religion in Estrangement

Education and religion have both been seriously impaired by their estrangement in Western society during recent times. This estrangement in one respect is the consequence of social development. Institutions become more specialized as society becomes more complex. Thus, institutional religion and institutional education must each be released from control by the other. Neither can do the work of the other, and neither must interfere with the other else the service of each will be seriously impaired. But institutional independence should not hinder close cooperation. Religion and education need one another. The conduct of human living suffers serious malady if each does not gain from the other what it needs. At present, our society is suffering from this malady. Education lacks the unifying aim and dedication of effort which the right kind of religious commitment would provide. Religion lacks the educated minds equipped to understand the deeper issues of religious concern and respond intelligently to the demands of a mature faith. Minds are educated, to be sure, but not concerning the religious problem. They cannot be until this problem becomes

---

[*] See Peter Drucker, *The Practice of Management* (New York: Harper & Row, 1954). See also by the same author, "The Promise of Automation," *Harper's Magazine* (April, 1955).

central to higher education. When minds are highly educated in all other areas but there is no intensive education equipping the mind to deal intelligently with the religious problem, the prevailing form of religion is immature and incompetent to shape the conduct of industry, government, education and the family and to set the major problems for intellectual search and artistic achievement.

This ineffectiveness of religion in providing a devotion to give direction to the whole of life may be obscured when people go to church in great numbers and practice religious ceremonial in vast multitudes. Popularity is not the same as depth, truth, and power in religious commitment. The numbers attending religious services and practicing religious commitment may render religion less effective instead of more effective *if* the commitment does not bring the lives of these people under the control of what actually has the power to shape the developments of society and course of history toward the ends of highest human attainment. A religion thus inefficient and deficient may be entirely sincere and fully devoted. Nevertheless, if what commands religious commitment is not what truly can shape society and the course of history and the life of the individual in ways of salvation and transformation, then the more sincere and free of hollow formalism is the commitment the more disastrous the error of this religion. Also, the greater the numbers who practice such a religion, the greater the harm it does.

The more complex the society and the more powerful the agencies to be controlled, the more free of error and confusion should be the intellectual understanding of what can save and transform when people give supreme devotion to it. Also, the more powerful and complex the society, the more dangerous are religious myths unless they can be translated into definite propositions subject to the tests which distinguish truth from error. This is necessary because without these tests we cannot know if the myth leads to futility or to strength, to error or to truth, to salvation or to destruction. Or again the myth may generate an exalted feeling ending in futility with no effectiveness either for good or for evil.

In a complex society with powerful agencies to be controlled by many people in responsible positions, these people should be equipped with intellectual understanding of the problems and issues of religion. If they are not so equipped the religion, if any, which they produce will be either ineffective or evil in its effects. Decisions made in government, industry, education, the family and the professions will determine whether we head toward disaster or move toward attainment. These decisions, in turn, will be shaped by the ultimate commitment ruling the lives of these individuals. This commitment is the religion actually practiced. It will be rightly directed to what saves and transforms creatively, or it will be wrongly directed, depending on what the individual sincerely believes concerning these matters.

The statement just made is intended to show that we have come to the time when general education, especially from high school on, must include intensive study of the religious problem along with study of the other problems determining the outcome of human life. With this understanding of the matter let us look at the change which automation will bring about in education. After that we can see what changes may be required in religion to cooperate effectively with education in meeting the demands of the new society.

Previous reference was made to the study of automation by Peter Drucker. He clears away misunderstandings about automation, such as the notion that it will cause unemployment beyond the transitions from one kind of work to another; or that it will reduce the significance of human work in industry to a place subordinate to the work of machines. Exactly the opposite will be the consequences of automation. Industry with automation will require more workers than it does now, but they must have an education more thorough and extensive than is ordinarily provided in our colleges and universities at present. Furthermore, the kind of work they do will be very, very different from what has heretofore been associated with labor.

Drucker quotes one large manufacturing company on this point. After making a study of the plant to see what changes would be required for automation the conclusion was reached that when automated the company would need seven thousand additional college graduates each year just to keep going. It must have much better educated people. The education required will not be training to do one special kind of work. It must be education which develops the powers of constructive imagination, initiative and insight in dealing with new problems and, above all, ability to communicate creatively so that you get the vision of the other person and she or he gets yours. "If there is one thing certain about automation," says Drucker, "it is that the job--even the bottom job--will change radically and often."

It is important to emphasize the contrast between learning in the sense of acquiring knowledge and skill and learning in the sense of creative interchange. In acquiring knowledge and skill without creative transformation of the mind, the perspectives and assumptions of the mind remain the same. One merely acquires more efficiency in dealing with the world as one interprets it with assumptions unchanged. These deep-laid attitudes of mind, which may not change when acquiring skill but do change with creativity, determine the kind of order which one finds in the world. They determine what commands one's attention and what one ignores. They determine what meaning sensations bring to the mind and thus the form of what one perceives. They limit the insights which can emerge and the range of imagination. Commitment to creativity changes these deep-laid attitudes so that the mind can discover a more inclusive order in the world, can give attention to what previously was ignored, can perceive forms of objects not accessible to consciousness with the unchanged attitudes, can have insights and ranges of imagination not possible until creative interchange occurred. Such is the difference between learning which is nothing more than acquisition of knowledge and skill and learning by way of commitment to creativity.

Thus learning without commitment to creativity does not develop the kind of mind which automation must have or the kind of mind able to meet the demands of responsibility in contemporary society. Education can be so ordered and conducted as to develop such minds, but this it can do far more effectively and extensively if institutional religion leads people to accept the sovereignty of this creativity over their lives. Otherwise the internal resistances of the mind to creative transformation cannot be overcome so fully and in many cases not at all. If institutional religion does cooperate in this way not only will it serve society, industry and the individual, but in this conjunction with industry and education it will acquire a power which religion has not exercised in our society for centuries.

Automation will not fail to demand minds educated for creativity; nor will education fail to strive to develop such minds. The danger is that religion will fail to do its part. Perhaps the fatal failure at the high points of civilization has always been in religion, with the consequence that people in responsible positions could not solve problems which had to be solved in order to uphold the complex social order. This failure brings on the destructive dialectic described in the previous chapter, while success in solving these problems keeps the constructive dialectic in operation.

Marks of Immature Religion

Since the chief threat hanging over us is the danger that religion will not develop the maturity needed to cooperate with education, industry, government and the family, let us look again at some of the marks of its immaturity. Unless we know what these are we cannot work to correct them; and correct them we must if the chief danger is to be averted.

One form of immaturity in liberal religion is to appraise affirmations in terms of optimism and pessimism. With this standard one inquires first of all if the affirmation is optimistic. If it is, evidence is sought for its truth. If it is not, evidence is sought for its error. This can be a fatal weakness causing the thrusting spearhead of advance to soften and fumble and fail, ignoring the dangers which must be mastered. Also, it is immaturity because, according to our previous analysis, maturity is measured by the ability to tolerate anxiety during the interval before creativity produces the insight and reveals the course of action to follow.

The test of one's commitment to creativity is whether one can continue with unfailing zeal and devotion in the face of failure and defeat. Due to the difficulty of their attainment the greatest creations come forth out of long periods of failure. Some individuals or groups may seem to win success immediately, but only because they reap where others have sown. However, success may never come because creativity is not almighty. But the greatest fulfillment in anyone's life comes after one's death in the lives of one's children or friends and associates, or in some institution one has served or in some other development of life which one has promoted. Such being the case, the crucial test of commitment is not success experienced but continued devotion in the presence of its opposite. The kind of religious optimism which cannot face obstruction and defeat displays an immaturity which weakens commitment to the point where it is unfit to deal with great things.

Another form of immaturity in religion is refusal to consider seriously any problem which cannot be presented in a sermon. Sermons have their important place, but the whole purpose of religion is not exhausted in providing material for fine sermons. Perhaps the most profound and difficult problems which concern religion cannot be treated in the church at all but must be studied in the universities when the religious problem is recognized to be an essential part of education. But the importance of these problems should be recognized by the church even when their treatment must be handed over to people of research and life-long devotion to study. Language has not yet been developed to deal with levels of reality of profound concern for the conduct of human living. The language, and with it the ideas, must be created before these matters can be presented in sermons or treated in popular discussion. The light touch, the happy manner, and the inspiring talk must be with us always, but there are depths not reached in this way. These depths must also engage our attention; to ignore them because they are "heavy" is a form of immaturity.

Another kind of immaturity found in liberal religion is to ignore everything which cannot be brought under the categories of reason. The opposite kind of immaturity is equally disastrous, found in forms of religion not liberal. This opposite kind appears in the claim that faith can give us a kind of knowledge beyond the reach of reason. This is false. However, mystery is with us and cannot be denied. Reason never does more than apprehend the abstract structure pertaining to concrete existing things and persons. The concrete reality itself always eludes reason, although the qualitative richness of it can be felt and sensed more or less when dealing directly with concrete existence. Beyond the concrete realities about which we can make true statements is the vast mystery about which no warranted statement can be made. A mature liberal religion will recognize this mystery beyond the reach of concepts developed to date. At the same time it will not fall into the opposite kind of immaturity; it will not affirm beliefs about this mystery when these beliefs cannot meet the tests of reason. No divine revelation, no faith, and no authority can reach where reason cannot distinguish truth from error.

Still another form of immaturity seriously weakens liberal religion. It is the tendency of many to think that ritual and ceremony and assembly devoted to the practices of commitment have no importance; that only instruction and incitement to practical action should have central place in the work of institutional religion. This error arises from a misunderstanding of religion itself. The ultimate commitment of religious faith will certainly drive to action in all walks of life. But the specific instruction and incitement for such action should ordinarily occur where it is to be performed, namely, in government and politics, in industry and economic exchange, in school and scientific research, in family and art, in neighborhood and casual interchange.

The one institution least fitted for instruction and incitement to practical action in the several areas mentioned, and best fitted for doing something else of equal importance, is the church. It is impossible to be intelligent, effective and constructive in action if the whole self is not given over as completely as possible to what transforms the mind in dealing with the problems of life. The practice of commitment to this end is the work of the church.

When individuals or groups rush out thinking they are equipped to make the world better because they have information and skill, but when they do not have the capacity for insight and appreciative understanding of other minds, folly and trouble arise. Yet some are impatient if they find the church engaged in ritual, ceremony, exhortation, and assembly designed not to instruct and incite to specific forms of action but instead intended to help the individual put himself or herself more completely into the keeping of the creativity which transforms the mind in such a way as to enable one to be more constructive in what one does.

We all suffer from inner constraints which hinder appreciative understanding of other minds, which prevent the emergence of insights revealing what needs to be done in the concrete situation, which limit the reach and comprehension of the constructive imagination. Fuller commitment and renewed commitment to what transforms the mind in a way to overcome these inner constraints is the purpose of public worship, and this is the distinctive service of the church in a mature liberal religion. Nothing is more important than this to enable the individual to act wisely and effectively; but it is not the same as specifying any one particular course of action which should engage the individual. These two should not be confused and should be allocated to different institutions. The service of the church is to equip the mind for wise action but not ordinarily to specify the kind of action.

Three Social Developments

After this review of immaturities to be overcome let us look again at certain social developments which call for a mature form of liberal religion and open the way for the exercise of its power. Three developments have significant bearing on this issue.

The first of the three is economic. The wealth of the wealthiest in the economy now developing is sustained and increased by continually increasing the wealth of all. Mass production and automation cannot operate effectively unless all the people have increasing ability to purchase what is produced. These forms of production require great concentration of wealth controlled by a few but at the same time a very great distribution of wealth in the hands of many. Not only must there be a wide distribution of material wealth but also a wide distribution of education and cultural privilege because otherwise the many highly equipped minds needed to operate industry will not be available. Also without education and culture, abundant consumption will become destructive.

When the wealth of the wealthiest depends upon economic abundance and cultural opportunity for all, the highest development and maximum effectiveness of education and religion become economic necessities as well as spiritual needs. Religious leaders have often scorned the economic as though it were not religious. Certainly economic interest and action can be unreligious. So also going to church can be unreligious. But the economic can be as religious as the ecclesiastical if religion is understood to be the devotion of one's life to providing the conditions for the operation of what has the character and power to save human beings as they cannot save themselves and transform them into the best they can ever become.

The development of social conditions which favor the union of economic interest with education and religion in a common devotion is a time of opportunity for a mature form of religion. There is no suggestion here that those who give their time to making money will suddenly become highly moral and religious any more than those who give their time to "churchwork" will suddenly become highly moral and religious. But conditions can be more or less favorable for the integration of the diverse interests of life under the sovereignty of a ruling devotion to what saves and transforms. If education and religion can do their part in cooperation with the developing economy, these favorable conditions can arise.

The second of the three developments mentioned is political. Political is here understood to include not only government but all organizations designed for the exercise of power. The power of the mightiest in the society now developing is sustained and increased by continually increasing the power of the many. The many different agencies of power under the responsible control of many different people must all work together if a few are to have supreme power. In a society as complex as ours and now becoming world-wide, power and responsibility must be very widely distributed because no small group can operate all the innumerable and diverse organizations of power, each of which is necessary to sustain the power of all the others and therefore also the power of those at the highest levels of control.

The third significant development of our time driving toward the widest possible distribution of wealth and power and cultural opportunity is the conflict now raging between Communism and the Western world. This conflict is painful and dangerous but it is forcing those with wealth, power and culture to distribute these as widely and rapidly as possible to all the peoples of the earth. This compulsion arises from the struggle of the two systems each to win as much of the world to its side as it can. The struggle forces each side to distribute wealth, power and culture because of the two developments previously mentioned. The wealthiest cannot retain their wealth nor the most powerful their power without this distribution. Consequently the struggle for dominant power compels the rivals to distribute as stated. Consequently the revolution in distribution of wealth, power and culture which would have occurred in any case by way of economic and political developments is being accelerated.

This world-wide social revolution accelerated by the conflict just mentioned magnifies the need for creativity in dealing with new and complicated problems. Also in the world today as society is now developing, nothing is more important than the kind of interchange which creates appreciative understanding across the barriers of diverse cultures, faiths, social systems, races and economic and political interests. The day has come for the kind of religion which directs the ultimate commitment of humankind to the creativity which transforms the mind in this way. This is the day of its opportunity and the day of its saving power if it will rise to the challenge.

The great transition is upon us from wide-spread poverty to universal abundance, from warring peoples to a world community, from international anarchy to a level of existence more gracious and understanding of human need than the past has ever known. The transition will either destroy us or be consummated. Religion carries the heaviest load of responsibility for deciding which it will be.

WIEMAN'S VISION
OF A FREE RELIGION

"The two most significant names of American theology today . . . are Henry Nelson Wieman and Reinhold Niebuhr."[*] George Hammar of Uppsala University, writing in 1938, made this correct observation, for Wieman and Niebuhr clearly stood out as the most significant American religious thinkers of the twentieth century. Whereas Niebuhr was providing a contemporary interpretation of orthodoxy, Wieman was taking a fresh approach to religious issues, applying the scientific method in developing an empirical theology for the age of Freud and "The New Physics."

Having spent four years studying and four years as a parish minister, Wieman decided to seek a doctorate in philosophy. The issue that dominated his concerns at Harvard was defined by Wieman as the problem of religious inquiry. His doctoral adviser was Ralph Barton Perry, with Wieman identifying strongly with Perry's epistemological realism. This epistemology placed primary attention on the actuality of occasions rather than on the ideas of occasions. Developing the approach of the empirical sciences so it could be applied to the problem of religious inquiry, Wieman began his scholarly career seeking to direct theology to

[*] George Hammar, *Christian Realism in Contemporary American Theology* (Uppsala, Sweden: A.-B. Lundequistska Bokhandeln, 1940), p. 72.

that which is actually at work in human experience transforming life in ways humans cannot do for themselves.

After graduating from Harvard, Wieman spent ten years teaching philosophy at Occidental College. It was during this time that another major influence came into his thought through his reading of Alfred North Whitehead's *Concept of Nature.* On this Wieman reports:

> When Whitehead's *Concept of Nature* appeared it fascinated me. One blistering hot and stupefying summer in Southern California I toiled for many days upon it. Strange how one can detect the greatness of a man's thought before everyone can fathom it and even before the thinker himself has developed the implications of it or rounded it out.[*]

In the *Concept of Nature* Wieman was influenced by the analysis of sense awareness as awareness of "the whole occurrence of nature." He was concentrating on the need to develop a more objective sense of the reality beyond one's immediate subjective experiences. The theological empiricism of Friedrich Schleiermacher emphasized subjective experience, and the psychological approach of William James tended to restrain inquirers from envisaging a more objective sense of reality beyond themselves. Wieman began to challenge theology to move beyond the confines of its past limitations to focus on the objective reality in nature on which humans depend for their salvation. This new direction was first developed in *Religious Experience and Scientific Method,* published in 1926. If Henry Nelson Wieman's contribution had been limited to this one publication, his place would still have been secure in the field of

---

[*] H.N. Wieman, "Theocentric Religion," *Contemporary American Theology,* edited by V. Ferm (New York: Round Table Press, 1932), Vol. I, p. 345.

constructive theology in American religious thought. Of course, Wieman's contribution was not so limited, for over the years his inquiry had grown and been elaborated in subsequent works, in which he attempted to give a more definitive interpretation of the objective datum of religious experience.

To understand the impact of *Religious Experience and Scientific Method,* people must let their imaginations return them to the theological climate of the 1920s, especially for those in the liberal tradition, with its primary focus on the issue of theism. The ethical movement in American religious thought had become so strong that for many years, prior to the 1920s, there was a rejection of any serious interest in the reality of God. American liberal religion had, in effect, become a form of religious humanism patterned after the human Jesus. By the 1920s, however, the search for the historical and human Jesus had been negated by biblical criticism. Without an avenue to the human Jesus, theism became the crucial issue. The argument centered on whether one could continue speaking of the existence of God as an objective reality.

To the issue of theism, Wieman spoke as a fresh voice. He did two things at this point. First, he redefined the question of theism, arguing that the question "Does God exist?" is not the right question. Wieman asserted that God is the Something in their environment--however defined--on which humans are dependent for security, welfare, and increasing abundance. The *true* question is "What is the character of this Something on which humans are dependent for salvation?" Wieman explains his purpose.

> My own purpose is a very earnest and a very serious one. It is so to formulate the idea of God that the question of God's existence becomes a dead issue, like the question of other inescapable forms of natural existence, and all our energies can be turned to living for God and seeking better

knowledge about God.*

The second thing Wieman did was present a method by which theology could understand the character of this Something. This method was essentially an adaptation of the method of the natural sciences to the study of religious experiences, establishing an empirical foundation for modern theology.

Wieman spoke to a particular situation in such a way that he made a dynamic impact on the American theological scene. It has been suggested that Wieman did for liberal American theology what Karl Barth had done for European liberal theology some years earlier. Both men attempted to turn theology away from the preoccupation with a religion of ideals and to direct theology to the sovereign and ultimate God beyond our human ideals. Possibly Reinhold Niebuhr could also be included in this comparison, as Niebuhr attacked a religion based on ideals and not on the sovereign God. This relationship of purpose is commonly overlooked, because their theological systems differ. Wieman used the new philosophy of organism and an expansion of the scientific method, whereas Barth and Niebuhr were oriented to a neo-Reformation mode of thought. The important thing is that all three approaches were carrying on an attack against philosophical idealism, especially in the form of religious humanism. This orientation directed all that Wieman wrote about religious inquiry and the religious life. Wieman contended that in this century humanity is undergoing great social changes that are forcing us to ask anew the basic questions of salvation. He attempted to assist people in finding the answer to this concern by (1) helping to define the religious quest in a new

---

* H.N. Wieman, *Is There a God?* (Chicago: Willett, Clark & Co., 1932), p. 276.

way, (2) continuing to sharpen his adaptation of the scientific method to religious inquiry, and (3) developing a more rationally intelligible doctrine of God.

The Religious Quest

From the beginning of his theological writing, Wieman viewed religion as a way of life in which humans seek and commit themselves to the God functioning within nature, society, and human experience in a saving manner. Religion is designated as a way of life in which humans try to find the adjustment to the conditioning factors of the environment that will yield the most abundant life. In essence, religion is our attempt to adjust to all the facts of human existence, including the superhuman (but not supernatural) possibilities, in such a way that we are being saved. The test of whether the religion is true depends on whether the results are such that humans better understand that which saves and are able to make the necessary adjustments to that which saves. Eventually, religion is defined as the human commitment to what people believe to be of such character and power that it will transform them as they cannot do themselves, that it will save them from their self-destructive propensities and lead them to the fullest life possible, provided they meet the requirements.

Another way to understand Wieman's perspective of the religious quest is in terms of the function of religion. In his early writings Wieman speaks of the function of religion as that of helping humans to create proper habit-formations and of giving humans a surplus energy for creative living. Later, he asserts that the function of religion is "to point the way of salvation."* The true function is not just to

---

* H.N. Wieman, *Intellectual Foundations of Faith* (New York: Philosophical Library, 1961), p. 80.

cause people to be more sensitive, but it is *to lead* them to commit themselves to the God who saves and *to lead* them to live the conditions necessary for this salvation.

Wieman's reflections on the religious quest brought him to a consideration of mysticism. Indeed, he concluded that for religion to perform its function, it must be basically mystical in form. But he defined mysticism in a unique way: "Mysticism is when there is a breakthrough in personality forms which are followed by the consummatory stage of higher integration."[*] For Wieman, religious mysticism is an attitude of responsiveness to the undiscovered possibilities of God. The mystical attitude is of untold value, because it engenders a striving to the unknown that nothing can daunt. The other major value of mysticism is that it produces a state of contemplation in which humans can be free from any limiting factors that older forms of faith might impose. This state of open awareness can lead one to a consummatory state of higher integration, a stage at which the meaning is a commitment to that which transforms, to that good not one's own, and to the supplying of the conditions under which this good may be most operative.

Wieman is concerned that there be adequate realization of the religious quest in the contemporary situation. He is not concerned that humans will cease to experience God; rather, his concern is that human understanding of God's will will become more and more inadequate for meeting the requirements of living in this complex scientific and technological age. For religion to be adequate in the present age, it needs to include all the insights that science and technology offer, and it must be truly mature, leading to a fulfilling

[*] H.N. Wieman, "The Problem of Mysticism," *Mysticism and the Modern Mind,* edited by A.P. Shernotte (New York: Liberal Arts Press, 1959), p. 23.

stage of genuine freedom.

Throughout his life Wieman remained critical of the old forms of religion still active, because he considered them inadequate for guiding people in use of the great power available through science and technology. What has happened is that the old forms of religion in today's situation have offered a distorted faith. For many, faith is no longer a commitment to God that demands we consciously experiment to live within the will of God; rather, faith has become assent to authorities, doctrines, ceremonies, and the status quo.

Supernaturalism is the dominant old form of religion that needs to be replaced, because it creates an illusion that cuts people off from the true God on which they depend for their welfare and increasing abundance. This illusion presented by supernaturalism is self-defeating, because it does two things: (1) It diverts energy and devotion from the actual problems of existence, and (2) it misdirects the devotion and the striving of humans to ends other than the will of God and its fulfillment in their lives. In essence, supernaturalism turns people away from the God they experience and away from understanding and fulfilling the will of God that is revealed in natural experience.

Wieman also rejected traditional liberalism as being inadequate, because "it tried to introduce the empirical method into religion by basing it upon religious experience but without making clear what was the nature of religious experience and how it was to be treated scientifically."* This often led to just another version of the subjectivism to which Wieman was so opposed. Instead, he sought "a true liberal religion." This liberalism is to be that of genuine religious inquiry--seeking to experience God, seeking to

* H.N. Wieman, *The Growth of Religion* (Chicago: Willett, Clark & Co., 1938), p. 248.

understand God's will, and seeking to commit one's life to God in such a way that one's actions are in accordance with God's will. It is because Wieman's view of religion asserts that the essence of religion is to ask the question how people are to be saved that this method is so important. Now we focus on how Wieman's method applies to religious inquiry.

Scientific Method and Religious Inquiry

Wieman employs the scientific method for the purpose of gaining knowledge of God based on natural experience. He contends that humans have experiences that can be termed religious. These experiences are religious because in them people experience a saving quality in life. There is Something within human experience that saves and transforms in ways in which people cannot transform themselves. This Something in human experience is God, by definition. Humans do not cause or foresee these experiences; nor do they hold directive power over them. Therefore, they are not the creators of them. These experiences are caused by Something that is outside of humans but which functions in relation to them. This Something produces the experiences, and the task is to determine the characteristics of God from the experience, and the necessary conditions for the optimal operation of this power, in order that humans can live in more adequate relationship with God. Wieman is saying that knowledge of God is not an end in itself, but that living in relation to God on the basis of knowledge is the desired end for religious inquiry.

Wieman contends that God "lures" humans by the religious experience into seeking knowledge through the experience of the God-human relationship. He calls this "lure" by the traditional names "the grace of God" and "the transformation by the Holy Spirit." God speaks to humans in their experiences, but it is their responsibility to use the scientific method to discover the implications of God's revelation and act on this information.

Wieman presents four steps in applying the scientific method to religious inquiry. The first step is to develop a theory or hypothesis that designates, for testing purposes, an experience as a religious experience. This step is most crucial, for until one has developed theoretical foundations one cannot attain knowledge.

The second step is to analyze the theory to determine the essential characteristics of the concept, religious experience. Experience designated religious can then be contrasted with other kinds of experience.

Based on this analysis, the third step is to develop any relevant implications. One must exercise care in designating the implications, because they will guide one's actions, as one attempts to live in a more adequate relationship with God, the central element in the experience. The final step is to test this theory in other experiences, especially those one considers possibly to be religious. This experimentation is carried out by observation and rational analysis. Wieman calls the knowledge gained a "perceptual event."

Because Wieman's presentation of these steps was not, in our judgment, sufficiently lucid, an illustration of how Wieman would relate the perceptual event of immediate experience to the perceptual events of the Christian tradition may be more helpful. From a particular experience one perceives that it is necessary to live in a new way, a way that demands one be transformed into a new person in order to be in an adequate relationship with God. Within Wieman's method this perceptual event can be related to the perceptual events of the crucifixion and the resurrection of Jesus and to the way in which these events affected the disciples. Apparently, Jesus was not the kind of messiah the disciples had hoped for. When Jesus was crucified "they reached that depth of despair which comes when all that seems to give hope to human existence is seen to be an illusion." * After about the third day the disciples perceived a new relationship with Jesus. The bonds of their earlier expectations were lifted, as they became transformed persons in a new relationship with the figure they now regarded as God the Christ. It was, according to this understanding, the creative power of God working in their particular religious experience that revealed to the disciples this perceptual event. One who perceives in a religious experience that one is being transformed into a new relationship with God can gain a deeper understanding of this perception by considering it in relation to this and other perceptual events of a religious tradition.

Having found that the characteristics of the immediate experience in question conform to the characteristics of other experiences, the next step is to make rational inference concerning the meaning of the experience under consideration. These rational inferences serve as guides for living and as insights to be included in other theories to be retested. Only after a theory has been examined and tested by observation and experimentation that is oriented historically, and rational inferences have been made, does a person have knowledge. When knowledge has been gained of a religious experience, it is knowledge of God. The experience comes first, but to have any useful knowledge about the experience, the scientific method must be employed. The scientific method not only enables a person to get knowledge, but it also transforms the character of one's experiences, because it transforms one's habit of response. One develops a scientific attitude toward the Something

---

* H.N. Wieman, *The Source of Human Good* (Chicago: University of Chicago Press, 1946), p. 444.

that transforms, which means that proper use of the scientific method in religious inquiry enables one to be more attune to the specific experiences in which God's revelations occur. For Wieman, the scientific method is used without any real effect unless there is a faith commitment. Gaining knowledge of the God-human relationship is important, but this knowledge is of limited value until one acts upon it, by making an absolute faith commitment to the power of God. Because knowledge of and commitment to God is the aim of the religious inquiry, based on the scientific method, we turn to Wieman's doctrine of God.

Doctrine of God

As indicated earlier, the theological problem of the 1920s was dominated by the question of demonstrating the objective existence of God. Wieman limits knowledge about God to the context of human experiences and the following of a proper rational method in examining these experiences. His line of reasoning is roughly as follows: All experiences are of objects. One has an experience that, for reasons we have outlined, one calls religious. By definition, God must be the object of this experience; therefore, God is an object that exists. The nature of everything that exists is to interact with other things. Because God is an object that exists, God must interact with other objects. When God interacts within human experience, humans are able to know God through this interaction. Wieman is saying that God can be known only as God functions in relation to humans.

To say that God exists is not enough; the distinguishing characteristics of God must be specified. In Wieman's view, for the word God to be used properly, it must refer to that which saves humans as they cannot save themselves; the word, properly used, does not refer to the infinite, omnipotent, and perfect, but actually to that which saves in human experience.

Wieman used a variety of terms to establish the distinguishing characteristics of God. Although his *essential* view of God did not change, his doctrine of God does reflect the theological shift from a cosmological to a more contextualist pespective utilized in later writings.

Wieman began by saying that God is that *process* in the universe which is Supreme Value, meaning that God is the Something upon which people are most dependent for their security, welfare, and increasing abundance. God may be much more than this, but God is this by definition.

In the *Methods of Private Religious Living,* God is presented as the "integrating process" at work in the universe, whether humans know of it or not. This process carries in its existence and in its possibilities the patterns that make possible the richest and most complete mutuality there can be. The nature of God is to function in the universe so as to bring about the greatest degree of mutuality possible. The responsibility of humans is to open themselves to God's functioning so that this mutuality can happen. Mutuality occurs when self-integration occurs, and when integration occurs with fellow humans, with God, and with the total universe to the greatest degree possible. This is salvation; it is the good; it is the highest value.

In *The Issues of Life,* Wieman developed the concept of God as the "order of greatest value." This concept expresses in another way the same theme of God as the integrating process but emphasizes the uniqueness and importance of communication. Through the use of language people come to understand themselves, their fellows, and the functioning of God. Language is the tool that makes possible the integrating process; for as language is properly used, the integrating process occurs. Thus, for Wieman, the order of greatest value is synonymous with the order of communication.

Eventually, Wieman shifted his focus even more fully from a cosmological to a contextual orientation. By this shift we mean that he became more concerned with analyzing the context of human experiences to see how God really saves instead of devoting all the attention to describing the Saving Something in the cosmological process. This shift is seen beginning in *Normative Psychology of Religion* and in *The Growth of Religion,* and is more clearly evident in *Now We Must Choose.* Here Wieman continues his discussion of God as the greatest value but stresses the need for humans to understand how God saves and the need for them to commit their lives to God.

God is now defined by Wieman as creativity, and God is to be identified only with that within the universe which is creative of human personality and its highest fulfillment. Although not rejecting completely the importance of cosmological considerations, Wieman claims the immediate demands of life are so crucial that time for such considerations is no longer affordable. God as creativity is to be understood as the character, structure, or form that enables the events of human life to be creative. Yet, creativity does not fully convey Wieman's intent. Therefore, he also speaks of God as the creative event. Wieman is always careful to make the distinction between the structure of an event and the process or function of the event in reality. Whereas God as creativity is the structure that makes goodness possible, the creative event is the character of goodness, the source of goodness that occurs in human life. If God were not this structure of creativity, the reality of the creative event could never occur and humans could not be saved.

Wieman is trying to assert that God is transcendent (creativity) and immanent (the creative event). Creativity is an abstraction that humans infer because of their knowledge concerning the immanence of God. The creative event is not an abstraction; it is the concrete reality in human experience that saves. He contends that the God of whom he speaks is the sovereign God working at the level of human, interpersonal relations. God as creativity gives a changeless structure to these interpersonal events so that the possibility of creativity can be realized. God as the creative event is the actualized reality of this possibility as it occurs in the event, transforming human understanding and appreciation, and thus saving humans. For Wieman, the whole process is seen in contextual terms. Humans have an important role in the creative event. Their responsibility is to open themselves to the source of God so they can be transformed. Practically speaking, people carry out this dedication by creating the attitudes or conditions that are necessary for life to be transformed continually, making it possible for the creative event to occur in each changing situation.

Perhaps above all, Wieman's theology is a radical affirmation of the sovereignty of God. It is a nontraditional version of the old doctrine, to be sure, but sovereignty remains the main theme. God as creativity works so as to create the conditions in which humans can be saved. God creates the environment and the mind of humans so that salvation may be a potentiality. The structure of God is such that the actual situations of reality become potentially saving situations. God redeems humans. They must open themselves to the situations God has created. When they respond appropriately to the situations God has opened, God transforms the mind, the heart, and the total being. God sustains individuals by meeting persons in the events of life in such a way that lives are continually being transformed. Humans must be responsible, as in the process of redemption, but it is God who sustains. God transcends individuals because God is and does more than an individual with limited perspective can ever know. The responsibility of individuals is to seek and nourish institutions and religious visions that will provide the conditions where the transforming work of this power can be successful.

Therefore, one sees Wieman's concern for the proper vocation of a free religion. It must nurture, not obstruct, creativity. It must sustain those elements of culture and of human interaction that serve to heighten and advance those sensibilities of grace and goodness and transformative power that, in Wieman's eyes, will always be seen as sovereign.

Creighton Peden
Larry E. Axel